Attention to the Mystery

paulist press

new york, n.y. and ramsey, n.j.

ATTENTION TO THE MYSTERY

Entry into the Spiritual Life

by
Yves Raguin, S.J.

translation by
Kathleen England, O.S.U.

Library of Congress Catalog Card Number: 82-60595

ISBN: 0-8091-2494-7

Published by Paulist Press
545 Island Road, Ramsey, N.J. 07446

Printed and bound in the United States of America

Contents

Preface

Since their publication, *Paths to Contemplation, The Depth of God,* and *The Spirit Over the World* have gone their way. They make up a trilogy that someone called a trinitarian doctrine for our times. Although very different in content and appearance, the three follow along the same lines. One day, after reading *Paths to Contemplation,* a young Chinese Jesuit said to me: "Father Raguin, now that you have brought out three books like this, you should die content." I hope to publish other books on spirituality, provided they are worthwhile, and so may claim a still happier death. I certainly get great joy out of these books, and they spur me on to write still more.

An author is always in danger of weaving continual variations on the same theme, exploiting unendingly a unique vein. It is impossible to bring out fresh ideas for sale all the time. To want to do so at all costs would risk turning out fiction instead of coming back again and again to reality itself, to explore its every facet. Now the divine life is within us. It is a reality and a fact surging up all around us and in us. To get at it there are hundreds of roads and thousands of ways. Some people are happy with large-scale maps while others need more detail and guides that point out everything. They want to know what this spiritual life is that people talk about so much while it is so hard to grasp and understand. They want to know where they are going as if to say: "Mysticism is beyond us. Just teach us how to live and understand our inner life."

This book was written to serve as a kind of basic text for friendly talks given in Chinese to Chinese students, which explains its analytic and didactic character. Its spiritual doctrine is identical with that in the above-mentioned trilogy, but many notions there taken for granted are explained here in detail.

This book, however, is not meant solely for beginners. It may shed light on the paths of those starting out as well as the more advanced, since basic principles are the same at all stages of the spiritual life. As in the preceding works, allusions to Chinese thought are fairly numerous and generally more explicit because the text has been written for Chinese people. Hopefully, in this way a gradual fusion of Chinese and Western spiritualities will emerge.

The plan of this book is simple. It follows the Christian tradition of the inner way but always side by side with that of Buddhism and Taoism. Often these ways will cross and intertwine, only to separate again in the light of Christ. Those who want to walk by Christ's light have nothing to fear. They will even be encouraged at seeing the efforts of their non-Christian brothers treading other paths.

Introduction

For centuries we have talked of the spiritual life and we have known very well what we meant. But now we have people beginning to ask the meaning of a spiritual life as distinct from the Christian life. And there are those caught up by the current of secularization who can no longer see very clearly how to distinguish between Christian life and mere human life. The latter will go so far as to proclaim that if you are totally human, you are, by that very fact, perfectly Christian.

This extreme position makes the Christian life no more than a well-filled human life, that is, a secularized Christianity. To fulfill our human vocation completely, then, would be perfect Christianity. Relationship with God they would not deny, but it is not exteriorized in acts of prayer or worship. Implicit in thought and behavior, it never blossoms into "religion."

Such a viewpoint, widespread among many Christians, is very similar to traditional Chinese thought. Confucianism recognizes relationship with heaven but it never expands into personal acts of religion toward heaven. In other words, Confucianism is a secularized religion. Religious acts were, in fact, reserved to the emperor as "son of heaven." The emperor's subjects were to pay homage to their ancestors, but personal relationship of man with heaven was not the object of religious attention. In this system, the inner life was concentrated on the exercise of human virtues, with little thought for relationship with

3

either God or heaven. I note this resemblance between modern religious secularism and Confucianism to throw light on our "spiritual life" problem.

This introduction will offer a first sketch of what the spiritual life could be if lived with a modern outlook—an introductory outline that will be gone into in greater detail later on.

1. Baptism and divine sonship

At baptism, every Christian receives a grace that establishes a previously non-existent relationship between himself and God. From being a child of God by creation, he becomes a son by participation in the sonship of the only Son of the Father; he becomes fully his child by participation in the personal sonship of the Word of God. The passage from one sonship to another comes about through baptism.

This human being remains as human after baptism as before. The grace he has received should not be looked on as "something" added to his human nature. What happens is that God offers man a closer relationship which we call participation in his divine life. It is similar to what takes place when an acquaintance becomes a friend or a friend becomes a husband or a wife. It is hard to say that the gift of friendship and then of love adds an element to the one who receives them, but something has changed in the nature of the relationship; it has become closer and more personal, as when Jesus said to the apostles, "You are my friends . . . . I call you servants no longer" (Jn 15:14-15). It is this kind of deepening that comes about.

Baptismal relationship is the essence of Christian life. Christ shares his sonship and man accepts it in faith. Henceforth, he is animated by a new but imperceptible life that remains a hidden current in the eyes of the Christian. Faith tells him of the ever-active divine life within, even if he is not expressly thinking of or adverting to it. All that is asked of him is to conform his behavior to the demands of this life, and he knows what this means through Christ himself, because that life is Christ's own. Christ's giving of his life is its explanation. In this matter St. John's Gospel is very valuable, because it enables us to have a better grasp of the meaning of the inner life that is ours through faith and baptism. Reflect, for example, on the conversations with Nicodemus and the Samaritan woman. There Jesus lets them glimpse the existence of an inner life that is God's own gift of life.

Essentially a relationship with God, this new life leads the Christian to match his conduct with its demands by listening to the words of Jesus in the Gospel.

Most Christians content themselves with a very simple way of practicing their religion by going to Mass and praying. They pray, sing, and receive the Eucharist because the Church tells them to do so. The inner mystery of their Christian life shows itself in these acts of piety and liturgy, but they never stop to think of its meaning. Their Christian life is simply a life of faith in action.

Such Christians may have very deep faith but their inner life stays buried. They may be closely united with God without taking much notice. They are living the great mystery of the divine life by instinct and knowing very little about it. They know what they should do and that their life is "in God through Christ," and that is enough for them. There is no pause to meditate on these mysteries, but they just live their Christian life and nothing more.

These Christians do indeed possess a life of relationship with God, but not consciously lived. The life is there without being the object of any special intention or attention. What they have to do they do, and that is how they live their relationship with God which they received in baptism.

Christians who go to Sunday Mass for mere form's sake are Christians more in name than in fact. The basic relationship with God is in them, but it is sterile.

Should a Christian, however, pay attention to the divine life in him, he will certainly possess an interior life. Recognition of his relationship with God is not merely a matter of outward acts but inner activity and deep attention to the mystery of the relationship with God which makes him Christian. No longer satisfied with acts, prayers and good works, he tries to remain attentive to the mystery of God's love for him, and this gives inwardness to his Christian living. No longer superficial, it becomes an inner Christian life.

The object of this inner attention is no less than the central mystery of the Christian life which is personal relationship with God. When a Christian having an interior life goes to Mass, he lives the mystery intensely in the depths of his heart, with a vision passing beyond appearances to reach the very center of the ceremonies and prayers.

This inner grasp is not added on from outside. A vision of the essential reality of the ceremony is meant to bring us to understand through signs that something is happening between ourselves and God. Being hidden like any other life, this relationship is perceived through signs that make us aware of the mystery of union going on in its depths. The inner life turns us inward to search for the true meaning of the mysteries unfolding before our eyes.

2. Interior life, spiritual life and relationship with God

Interior life and spiritual life are practically synonymous. The concept of spiritual life implies attention to the things of the spirit as distinct from the flesh and the senses in general. But spiritual life and intellectual life should not be confused either. A person who concentrates his intellectual capacities on the Christian life may have only a very weak spiritual life. To intellectualize the Christian life is not necessarily to live according to the Spirit.

Always implied in the definition of the spiritual life is attention to relationship with God. Possessed by every man, it becomes closer and more personal in the Christian, as Louis Cognet asserts in *Les problemes de spiritualite*:

> There is spiritual life when there is relationship with God. Thus we might say that interior life and spiritual life are the same thing, though these two are not exactly synonymous even if they tend to

mix. We should say, then, that there is spiritual life when an inner activity organized around personal relationship with God is present. Hence, the different manifestations of this inner life, whether the Mass we assist at, the rosary we recite, the half-hour daily meditation, etc., all come, in the final analysis, to activating that personal relationship that by grace and within our Christian life we are able to have with God.

On the dust-jacket of the book I have just quoted is this phrase which I consider an excellent definition: "The spiritual life consists in living a personal relationship with God." That such exists does not necessarily imply an existing spiritual life. For this, the relationship has to be lived. Now this supposes awareness, and, then, concentration of all our human acts toward understanding and actualization of the relationship with God.

It is a question of life, so reflection or mere curiosity is not enough. We have to live the reality of the divine life in us, and living includes the whole man—intelligence, sensitivity, etc. Spiritual life should not be taken to be a kind of appendix to human activity. No doubt, it covers the entire field of this activity, but it is on a deeper level. Here, in fact, as I have already said, the word "spiritual" should be understood as "relative to God." The Spirit, in an absolute sense, is God, and the life is called spiritual because it is religious and directed toward God.

In short, basically the spiritual life will be attention to the mystery of the divine life in us, a conscious realization of our relationship with God. All practices that enable this inner life to grow will flow from this basic attitude: efforts to explore through Gospel study and Christian teaching to conform to Christ, contemplate and reach union with him.

This goes a long way to explain the gradual build-up over the centuries of theories and techniques of spiritual life. All the great religions have done the same thing to help their followers to actualize the mystery of their inner life. It is impressive to see the vast collection of doctrines on the spiritual life in Christianity, Buddhism, Hinduism, Islam and many other religions, for this teaching has been the great preoccupation of the most religious men throughout the centuries.

But for us in the twentieth century it is hardly possible to simply accept what we have inherited from the past. We have to probe the problem of the spiritual life in the context of our own times. Today the reality of the spiritual life is being challenged; many people no longer see how such a life can have anything to do with men of our scientific age.

Actually, the tendency is to intensify relationships with our fellowmen, leaving aside direct relationship with God. People repeat, truly enough, that the love of God is manifested through love of man. But then they go on to say that this love cannot be shown in any other way. Such a position excludes all direct relationship with God since, outside love of others, there would be no way of expressing it. This amounts to saying that God could not be reached otherwise than through relationship with our fellowmen.

The consequences of such an attitude are vast, for it refuses to admit the possibility for anyone to live a contemplative life of union with God. At a single blow it destroys the mystical, charismatic ways of the Christian world. Direct access to love of God would be barred. And it is a fact that since these ideas have become widespread, many people have abandoned prayer, contemplation and all that could be looked on as a search for personal relationship with God. On account of these theories, many have lost the call to greater personal closeness with God, and many have left the religious or priestly life altogether.

Hence, the problem of the spiritual life is vital for the modern world. This life needs to be seen in a fresh light that demonstrates its value and necessity. What is at stake is liberation for those who wish to live more intensely and openly the mystery of their personal relationship with God.

These few pages will try to throw some light on basic problems regarding this question. While not being exhaustive, their doctrinal and practical content may help some to clarify their ideas.

3. Interior life without explicit relationship with God

What has been stated so far places the spiritual and inner life in the setting of relationship with God. But there are methods of interior life and meditation that have nothing religious about them; that is, they make no objective reference to God. Their aim is to provide means for development of the deeper personal capacities, culture of human personality and growth of hidden potentialities.

Such, for example, is the objective of Transcendental Meditation. Although religious in origin, the master, Maharishi Mahesh Yogi, offered a non-religious version of ancient Yogic practices that has become very popular.

Methods of mental control and awakening to deep capacities such as these are as old as mankind, but they have developed especially in India with Yoga and in China and Japan with Zen. Confucianism has also known its self-culture methods which are completely non-religious. Very elaborate methods have come through Taoism for the nourishment of vital energies. For the Taoist this means good health and self-healing through the power of this vital energy that may also be used on others. Healers usually draw on such powers which they maintain by meditation. This, it seems, gathers together the general scattered energies in order to reach states of super-consciousness, which can result in healing or, simply, encouragement for others. Persevered in, meditation can lead to what are called magic powers. But all this is not yet, strictly speaking, an inner activity of religious nature connecting with the world of the spirit and the divine.

It must, therefore, be clear that exploration of the psyche and spiritual reality of man may go far without necessarily reaching that religious sphere which implies relationship with the spiritual world lying beyond. So long as a man is searching merely for expanded personal depth, his is not a truly religious attitude, even though, by the implied attitude, it is so analogically. The shallower self awaits the revelation of a deeper self, both being different levels of the same self.

The passage from ordinary to deeper consciousness usually produces a shock that may be called discovery, illumination, or depth-experience. The result is an awakening to the hidden wealth of the human being that brings with it a sense of extraordinary joy, peace and plenitude, often so great that it seems there is nothing left to be desired; there is a feeling of unity with the universe. Everything is contained in this oneness of a profound nature and in its unity all is totally present. On the one hand, it is a perception of emptiness, and, on the other, total plenitude. Those who experience this do not immediately, and sometimes never, discover that such plenitude is wholly self-centered and essentially limited. One day or other they will have to awaken to this boundary.

For whatever the sense of fullness experienced in the depth of my being, I am unable to explain to myself what I am or where I come from. The plenitude I perceive will end by seeming relative to another absolute plenitude. Only the limitation of my capacities for being makes me think I am everything and there is nothing else. Should I penetrate to the utmost my unity and identity, someone else will rise up in whom nothing relative subsists. Grasping my identity will reveal the difference, and the Other will be the key to my own identity. So, then, if I plunge into the depths of my own interiority, I shall learn that it is not self-subsistent but takes its origin from elsewhere. When I have traveled the human way, suddenly there will be an opening out to the divine, and then my journey will become totally religious.

In this perspective this book was written. It speaks of an interior and spiritual life open to God. Without pretending to exhaust so vast a question, these pages will present a few of the more important aspects of the spiritual path of a Christian who seeks to follow Christ a little closer.

I

Relationship with God
and
Attention to
This Relationship

As has been said in the introduction, to have a spiritual life is to live one's relationship with God consciously. A more roundabout definition would be to describe it as a life polarized by the recognition of our relationship with God and its development through prayer, meditation, and the sacraments.

Set in a still wider context, the spiritual life might be defined as awareness of the relationship with God whose love has been revealed to us by Jesus Christ. This definition places Christ's role in the forefront because he was the one to teach us what the spiritual life really is. In fact, when he showed his own relationship with the Father to his apostles, he showed it to us too. He lived out this relationship in front of his apostles so that they might grasp through his concrete daily life just how it was to be perceived and lived.

1. Spiritual life: attention to our relationship with God

Any objective reading of the Gospel shows that Christ's life is not directed solely toward his disciples and other men.

11

Christ comes back again and again to what makes him Son, that is, the basic relationship that makes him what he is. Suppress this and all the rest is nothing but a whiff of smoke.

Now every spiritual life first seeks for awareness of the basic link that makes us sons of God. In so doing Christ is our model and we have his own inner journey for our following. For it is impossible not to be struck by Christ's inward attention to his Father. No anxious preoccupation is to be found in it, for it was pure expression of what he, in fact, really is.

What is more, Christ never put this inner journey forward as if it were in any way opposed to his dealings with men. Moreover, he most certainly never taught that human relations should play down direct relationship with his Father. Now this is where we are in the thick of present-day polemics, because many people so stress love of neighbor that they toss aside the commandment to love God as if it were superfluous and out-of-date. No doubt, the touchstone of our love of God in the concrete is love of our fellowmen, but this by no means signifies that the second commandment has replaced the first. To set them up in opposition is foolishness, since they are inseparable: they are like two sides of the same coin.

This brings us to a vital question. God gave us existence when he created us in an act of love. Does this mean, then, that we have to respond to love by love? In other words, are we meant to love God with a love that responds to the love he had in creating us? For it is this essential love that created a direct link between God and us. If we recognize this link, is it not the same as when Christ recognized the link binding him to his Father? Contrariwise, are we not called by God to live out our human life as it comes without worrying too much about him?

Some theologians and exegetes claim that the Old Testament manifests a secularizing process of religion, which is very true. When the Jewish people received God's revelation, the gods who until then had filled the universe were thrust into the background, preparing the way for a religion that shifted the emphasis from ritualism to recognition of the divine action in history.

Christ came to stress some of these tendencies by opposing the Judaic culture that was losing its meaning before the inflowing of worship of God in spirit and in truth. In a way, then, the destruction of the ancient religious forms went on, but Christ had thrown a totally new light on the inner relationship of men with God. Now this is the very foundation of religion.

Those who speak only in terms of secularization back up their theory with the process they find in the Bible, but they carefully omit the passages where Christ throws wide open the religious world of relationship with the Father. This is not simply a man's recognition of his beginning, but his acknowledgement of his divine origin and eternal sonship, which is a strictly religious perspective.

Anyone with an inner life will listen to what Christ says of himself. As he disclosed the mysteries of his inward life to the apostles, he was opening the door to what we call the spiritual life insofar as it is distinct from an ordinary Christian life.

The apostles were intimately united with Christ, and he tried to enlarge their understanding of the mystery they were living. He was well aware that for the moment they could not grasp everything. But the Holy Spirit would come and teach them what had yet to be learned. This explains why the Spirit plays such an important role along every spiritual way. The Spirit is the love of Father and Son and their mutual bond. He is the one who unites man to God and awakens him to the understanding of this relationship. In a word, the Spirit is the master of the spiritual life.

2. Attention to God and attention to man

It is hard to comprehend any kind of Christianity that does not include this attention to the fundamental relationship with God. People should cultivate this attention so as to live by it, but many actually tend to think it quite superfluous. What God wants from man, they hold, is that he be a man and nothing more, without trying to meet God in any kind of personal relationship.

Clearly, certain extreme present-day currents of thought contradict that inner gaze Christ taught us in the Gospel. God could certainly have created the world in such a way as to ask neither our attention nor our love. But if Christ's coming still has a meaning, the inner search which is the very aim of the spiritual life must also have one. It would even seem to possess more significance than ever, since it provides a Christian interpretation for that characteristic of our times: concentration on man and the world he lives in.

Attention to God developed by the spiritual life should not deflect our gaze from the world and from men. On the contrary, precisely because it is at its very heart, it is there that it should expand and develop. The force of attraction drawing us to one another is an essential relationship woven into the very fabric of our human existence. But at a deeper level still there is a divine milieu where the core of this humanity has its root. This is that living space where our human milieu is plunged into the divine milieu by which it lives. The filaments that unite us are woven at this depth; we are all alive with the same life that generates the same pulsation and the same breath. To say that the human milieu is immersed in the inner divine milieu is not, strictly speaking, exact, because it is more a question of interior animation and infusion of life, grace and love. And this is the depth at which human beings are able to reach true understanding and love. The human setting of the most radical understanding and love is wholly buried in, and animated by, the divine milieu.

These considerations will be dealt with later, but we can foresee already how attention to men should lead to God and develop in us fresh love. There is no real opposition between God and the present trend toward rediscovery of the human. It would be illusory to suppose that what is human basically distances us from God. If our aim is to run away from him, obviously the deeper we delve into the human the more we are led away from him; the "distancing" is then the result of our own blind plunging.

What is human is only an obstacle if I stop halfway. But if I keep trying to analyze it to see where it comes from and

where it is going, I inevitably end up where I began—in God.
Ultimately, the world and matter can only reveal the deep
inner bond between themselves and the spirit of their origin.

A general view of existence and the universe brings us
back to what Christ came to tell us in ordinary, everyday
language anyone could grasp: between God and his world,
and men in particular, there exists a close relationship. Our
task is to get to the bottom of the kind of love God wants to
manifest in his creation, in mankind and in each one of us in
particular. Anyone who tries to be especially attentive to this
mystery of the world looks for ways and means to do so, and
this will be the object of his spiritual life. To actualize this
life, Christ, who opened up the paths leading to the Father, is
our model.

3. Man's link with God
and the relationships it implies

Through Christ we have become aware of a world of
already existing relationships between ourselves and God,
and of further potential ones he invites us to invent.
Precisely because of our basic existential bond with God, all
others have become viable. Without this real link between
God and ourselves, our spiritual life would be nothing but a
figment of our imagination. A whole book would be needed to
explain why we believe in this substantial relationship, but
since it is fundamental, we shall touch on it briefly, drawing
on Scripture and other religious traditions.

The Book of Genesis shows us God creating man by
breathing into him his own breath of life, an imaginative
way of conveying our essential relationship with God. He
has brought us into being in the power of his breath, the sign
of his animating and unifying Spirit. Existence has come to
us by an energy emanating from God, a creative power that
did not end there. Continually being created anew and put
into existence, our history is nothing but a manifestation of
the eternal. While totally autonomous in its own order, at a
much deeper level it remains relationship with God.

In this perspective we are able to conceive the possibility of God's communicating with man, and man reaching out to God. No doubt many people find this a stumbling block. For us, however, it is a fact, and what we name God's initial act of creation does not end here. This we express when we say that the act of relationship that gave us being is on-going and unending. For any being apart from God, existence is dependence, and dependence is relationship.

We are attached to God by the very ground of our being, and it is there that essential relatedness between man and God comes about. From it flows every other possible relationship in the same way as our acts issue from our being as such.

When it comes to existence, reality precedes theory. It seems hard to deny the existence of a reality to which we ourselves are obviously the closest. Aware of our fleeting, limited condition in being, we find it difficult to envisage it in other but contingent terms. So we agree, with probably the greater part of mankind, that there exists something that is non-contingent and absolute. But here again we are up against a problem: How can what comes from the absolute be anything but absolute itself? Human reason gets us nowhere. Yet it seems more normal, on the whole, to admit of an absolute producing a contingent and limited being rather than the contrary, that is, the absolute issuing from the contingent. The latter, then, remains dependent on the absolute which is basic to, and built into, relationship.

The Bible is our guide in the study of creation and human history. From the very start, man appears to be called by God himself to accept his fundamental dependence freely. This acceptance was meant to be the most weighty act of human liberty. A man who posits this basic act can no longer say that existence has been forced on him. It follows that he should freely accept his relationship with God. Throughout the history of the people of Israel, God was working to lead man gradually to the point of total and free acceptance of his destiny and history. And when Christ came to reveal his relationship with the Father and call us to the heights and perfection of his filial obedience, we had in him a perfect model.

As we have it in Scripture, the history of salvation is an ascension toward an ever-increasing personal relationship to be set up between God and man, culminating in love. As Christ says to Nicodemus: "God so loved the world that he gave his only Son" (Jn 3:16). Love shown in giving implies a love-relationship, and Christ would reveal this in depth at the Last Supper.

To grasp the meaning of this love-relationship, we should compare it with the basic notions of some other religious philosophies. The greater number of these systems look on the Absolute as impersonal or transpersonal. Man comes from it as an emanation, though it is not easy to envisage an authentic relationship existing between man and this Absolute. The same kind of bond exists between man and the Brahman in Hinduism or with the Tao in Taoism.

But since man finally craves a personal relationship with God, Hinduism has developed the cult of the divinities of Brahma, Vishnu and Shive as manifestations of the impersonal Brahman. In certain forms of Hinduism, devotion is centered on the cult of these divinities even though they are taken to be inferior to Brahman who remains unique and beyond all personal determination.

Because of the exceptionally rich and complex nature of his myth, Krishna merits separate treatment. Compared with the beauty and noble features of this figure, Christ may seem to be at a disadvantage and appear to lack brilliance and fascination. But for the Christian this is, perhaps, precisely the point. Christ in his incarnation is more a man than all the great non-Christian divinities. Myths have their value, no doubt, but nothing outweighs God made man, a fact truly surpassing all myths. The spiritual life of the Christian is thus based on a human reality so concrete that we might even hesitate to realize all its implications.

Taoism has the same problem as Hinduism with regard to the Absolute and its manifestations. Philosophical Taoism holds that all existing things reveal the Tao, whereas in religious Taoism there is a disclosure of the Tao in three distinct personal manifestations, usually named the *San Ch'ing*, the Three Pure Ones, or *T'ien-tsun*, Venerable

Ones of Heaven. There are many lists, among which the generally accepted one in Taoist milieus is Yuan-shih T'ien-tsun, Ling-pao T'ien-tsun, and Tao-te T'ien-tsun. The first represents the creative aspect of the Tao, the second his manifestation as sanctifier and giver of immortality, and the third his active aspect, or the "Tao in action."

Here we touch on a basic factor in the theory of relationship to the Absolute. In these systems, relationship with God cannot have the same personal character as in Christianity. If Christ were not God but a mere human, we might be in the same predicament. We could then have personal relations with Christ and through him "touch" God but God himself would be forever out of reach of any sort of interpersonal relationship.

Fundamental to the doctrine or relationship with God in Christianity is the fact that in Christ we are relating, not to a mere manifestation or image of God, but to God himself. The heart of this doctrine was gradually revealed by Christ as he unveiled his privileged relations with God the Father and Origin of all things; then one day he said "I am," using the very expression used by God himself in the Old Testament to reveal himself to Moses (Ex 3:14; Jn 8:28, 56). And he added: "The Father and I are one" (Jn 10:30).

We may conclude, then, that in other religions the very mystery of the Absolute has remained blocked whereas in Christ we are admitted to "know" the inner life of God. Through him we see to what depth our inner gaze is invited to penetrate and to what mystery we should be attentive.

4. Attention to relationship with God

Here we can once more take up the definition of the spiritual life which was mentioned in our Introduction and deepened by what has been said. The spiritual life consists in living our relationship with God which, we have seen, does not leave us simply at God's outer fringe. Were this so we should have merely to remain in silent fear and admiration, mute before the impenetrable mystery of God. This attitude does actually exist in Christianity but it is only a stage. The

Chinese would call it *ching*, that is, the reverent, respectful attitude and profound attention to the mystery.

This inner attitude can only be reached through the purifying and unifying peace expressed by a further concept which is another *ching*, namely, "silence, calm, deepest quiet." While the second notion signifies an inner attitude, the first refers to attention to the hidden mystery.

When the mind has reached this point it is already settled and fixed in contemplation. Such concentration is defined as, *ting*, "fixation," a concept to be found in ancient Chinese thought. Buddhists have made use of *ting* to translate their notion of *samadri*, which is "total absorption of thought in the act of meditation." At this stage the mind is ready for the final intuition, enabling it to grasp the unknowable mystery as far as is possible.

What has been sketched up to now is roughly the road that should be taken by anyone aiming at attention to the mystery of his relationship with God through a "spiritual life." Awareness of our unifying relatedness to God means that we have to build up a certain number of acts of contact such as adoration, thanksgiving, intercession and participation in the Christian mysteries. These are acts of relationship, that is, they express a link. We have acknowledged that we are bound to God and have accepted this link, which we signify through a number of personal or communitarian acts. There are Christians who have a more vivid realization of their relationship to God and they feel the need to be continually and deeply mindful of him. In a word, they think such a manifestation of God's love demands on their part a far greater attention.

5. Spiritual life and state of life

In this area there is a vast amount of freedom, all depending on God's inspiration. Some people will stay in the world and marry. They will try to live a more intense Christian life, and, without being odd, they will add freely a certain amount of prayer, reading and meditation, seeking to become more responsive and conscious of the demands made by their relationship with God. In its Dogmatic Constitution on the Church (*Lumen Gentium*, 31), Vatican II has sketched an excellent portrait of the layman who has understood his relationship with God.

> The laity, by their very vocation, seek the kingdom of God by engaging in temporal affairs and by ordering them according to the plan of God. They live in the world, that is, in each and all of the secular professions and occupations. They live in ordinary circumstances of family and social life, from which the very web of their existence is woven. They are called there by God so that by exercising their proper function and being led by the spirit of the Gospel they can work for the sanctification of the world from within, in the manner of leaven. In this way they can make Christ known to others, especially by the testimony of a life resplendent in faith, hope and charity.

More explicitly, the Decree on the Apostolate of the Laity (*Apostolicam Actuositatem*, 4) speaks of the spirituality of the laity and their vital union with Christ.

> This life of intimate union with Christ in the Church is nourished by spiritual aids which are common to all the faithful, especially active participation in the sacred liturgy. These are to be used by the laity in such a way that, while properly fulfilling their secular duties in the ordinary conditions of life, they do not dissociate union with Christ from that life. Rather, by performing their work according to God's will they can grow in that union.

There will be others who will live a life of consecrated celibacy, in the world, in religious life or in the priesthood. Celibacy is in itself a response to God's call to greater intimacy. This of course can be reached in the married state. But it would seem that there is one type of intimacy that blossoms only in celibate life. Today, a good deal of stress is laid on the fact that human love fulfills a man and gives him greater understanding of loving and giving. True enough, but it does not follow that a celibate necessarily lacks maturity. In fact, the harvest of a certain grasp of loving, giving and relationship with God and man is reaped in celibacy as well.

How then is the choice of either state to be made? It is a personal matter based on tastes and aspirations that may not always be understood. Nowadays we say that celibacy is of the charismatic order. This is a way of expressing the fact that it escapes any ready-made slogans such as: "Marriage is the normal way," "Marriage is the school of self-giving," "The love of God can only be manifested in the mutual love of husband and wife." These viewpoints that tend to prevent free choice should be quietly reacted against. The Spirit is ever-active and still inspires some men and women to consecrate themselves to God in this way by giving their inner life a very specific expression.

6. Truth of the spiritual life

The spiritual life will give rise to a certain number of inner attitudes and practices, prayer and meditation, that are the expression of a person's awareness of his relationship with God. There will be as many types of expression as there are personal tastes—silent adoration, meditation, contemplation, etc.—but the central core is always the same: awareness of this relationship

The spiritual life, then, is going to be bound up with an intense psychological activity, for all that bears on relationship with God will take shape in our consciousness and have an after-effect on our intellectual and affective activity. This gives rise to a fresh basic problem which must be dealt with briefly.

Non-believers, and a good many believers too—among them some Christians—will say that this is all sheer imagination. Anyone who goes on for an interior life is living in a dream-world. He is projecting his inner cravings

and building a so-called but non-existent spiritual world
where he can take refuge from hard realities. There is no
denying that such types do exist. But is this the same for a
spiritual life firmly constructed on concrete human
existence?

The very people who are living a truly authentic inner
life quite often put this same problem to themselves. "How
can I know," they ask, "if my impressions of love of God are
not products of my imagination and feelings? I experience
strong sentiments of love of God, but how am I to know if
they are not illusions? At times it seems as if God makes his
presence felt, but how is it possible? I am afraid of taking my
feelings for divine lights."

We should first recognize that, before possessing a
conscious, psychological life, a man exists. His psychological life is built up slowly like the growth of a child gradually
taking in and becoming aware of himself and the world
around him. A man already "exists" in a specific and very
personal way before he knows what he is or is able to express
it. The fact of existence, then, is anterior to thought and
feeling.

Now the fundamental and primary relationship of man
with the divinity is constitutive of his being. Existentially,
historically and even logically, the relationship is anterior to
all psychological functioning. Ontological relationship, that
is, in "the very being itself," has been deepened by Christ's
coming. The new relationship is also ontological, but it
penetrates being at far greater existential depth, binding it
to the inner life of God in a person-to-person relationship.
The bare fact of existence is this primary relation that makes
the being made alive by God "to be." Christ then brings his
gift of grace, enabling us to live in a fresh existential
relationship with God that deepens the first by revealing the
perfection of personal relationship with him.

After speaking of psychological activity in *Les problemes de spiritualite*, Louis Cognet sums this doctrine as
follows: "What I hold is that this person-to-person relationship between God and man starts by existing and only then
becomes real on the level of conscious, psychological

activity. My inner life is relationship with God; but it is my inner life because I am aware of it. I know it exists and hence sets in motion the various elements of my psychological activity."

From the very beginning of existence, then, there is a relationship that man has discovered mainly through Christ's revelation. Later will come the attempt to express it in human terms, and finally there will be man's response to the one who is origin and partner in the relationship.

No man can fully grasp our basic relationship with God. Nonetheless, since it is constitutive of our being, we have an obscure perception of it within the human reality of our existence, above all because of the impossibility of explaining ourselves to ourselves. This basic powerlessness is what ultimately causes us to sense a relationship with God. Men have scrutinized this mystery without getting to the bottom of it, and yet they learned to understand that their existence was "relationship." More often than not they looked on it as a kind of "fate," *ming*, but very rarely as love.

Christ was the one to bring us the revelation of a personal relationship of love in the language of men. Being God and man, he could gauge the strength and effect of his words and enable them to contain the mystery. Christ's words should be interpreted in the light of the Spirit of Christ himself, who illumines their meaning from within.

7. Criteria of the spiritual life

We have always to confront our experience on the psychological level with Christ's expression of this relationship. But in each individual case the attitude of the spiritual man has to be examined carefully to see if he is not deluding himself. He has Christ's words and actions to go by, as we have seen, but for the interpretation to be correct, he needs also to listen to the Church and a spiritual guide. He has to be helped to discern rightly amid the variety of his ideas, feelings, spiritual experiences, desires, and practices.

A spiritual man does not have to limit his psychological activity to forging a spiritual world for himself, but he must

try to discover a total human expression of his relationship
with God. Everything must be included: a whole universe of
thoughts, sentiments, actions, etc. Far from being some
make-believe, it will strive to be the most authentic language
of a reality steadily growing in time.

Although it may be difficult to discern the criteria, true
spiritual experience usually carries with it the mark of its
own authenticity. To this end we need to be very clear
ourselves about the language God uses to "speak" to us, in
other words, to make us aware of the relationship he has set
up between us.

A man truly experienced in the ways of the spirit can
bear witness to the fact that, far from being deluded by his
imagination, his experience of God is a response to God's
call, or, again, the human expression of this relationship.
Such a man lives and analyzes the relation out of his human
experience, but he knows that this corresponds with God's
way of approaching him. God's love for man existed always,
and he never ceases manifesting it to mankind. This is what
a man discovers in a real experience of the divine if he is
willing to dig deeper into the reality of his Christian
existence. God has created the link—and no flight of human
fancy has invented it.

II

Life in Faith

The spiritual life is expressed in contemplation, reading of Holy Scripture or the great spiritual writers, and an inner attitude persisting throughout all life's activities. For some people, actual time given to contemplation may be reduced to a minimum; what should never be diminished is awareness of relationship with God. A spiritual life could be envisaged that no longer needed "times" of prayer or contemplation, a life that has become one long gaze on the mystery of God's love perceived in everything. Yet Christ himself, whom no one could accuse of not being united with God, went off sometimes to pray in solitude. His first objective was not to give his disciples a lesson. But, being man, he expressed his union with God and his inner life humanly by giving time to his relationship with the Father. It was not needed, one might think, since he was man-God. However, he was really and truly a man. He needed prayer, not only as a human expression of his relationship to the Father, but to bring this relationship to maturity and fullness in his humanity. He needed it, too, because in him the manifestation of the divine life was caught up in an historical development.

Although this is not the subject of the present chapter, it does lead us to conclude that the spiritual life, expressed in a whole series of practices and, above all, attitudes, is focused on attention to the relationship of love that unites us to God, and this attention is the expression of an act of faith.

Thus, the spiritual life springs from an act of faith in the reality of a relationship with God revealed through Christ and made achievable in him. The paradox of this experience of God is that it is lived wholly in faith.

Every Christian life is based on faith, the importance of which stands out above all when the spiritual life begins to grow. Then it is that we have to consolidate still more the reality of what we believe and ground our course on the truth of our relationship. Not even mystical experience may do away with the essential exercise of faith that leads to endless outdistancing of what we have reached by experience.

1. Faith and the perception of the goal of relationship

We have defined the spiritual life as an attention to relationship with God or again as living a personal relationship with God. But as Louis Cognet says very pertinently in the above-mentioned work, "While, in the human experience of relationship, the existence of another is of itself a vital object of certitude in religious experience this relationship remains a faith-affirmation. Whatever the value and level of a soul's experience, it must ultimately be dependent on faith."

Before starting an analysis of the act of faith, we should bear in mind that human relationship is based on trust that in its turn depends on an act of faith. For, although the existence of the person we relate to is an object of direct perception and a vital object of certitude, his sincerity and final attitude toward us are, in a very real sense, perceptible only in an act that is equivalent to an act of faith. The anxiety of love lies precisely in wanting to find through signs and witness a certitude of love itself, that is, of the total and unconditional gift of the person. There has to be an ultimate decisive act of trust that gives the one to the other. But how is this certitude to be reached? Violent passion is not the answer, because it does not necessarily express total giving. So what can be our criterion? Each individual will have his own. But some will never reach certitude because they fail to recognize signs that enable them to trust fully.

The initial evidence of love draws to deeper knowledge. Should there be no response to this first step and those that follow, reciprocal confidence will be blocked. Penetrating the meaning of a gesture or word will be the outcome of a first response. The person who receives the invitation should give a sufficiently authentic committed response to be able to grasp the meaning of that invitation. This should produce provisional trust. With further experience this will turn into confidence as the two learn to know each other. Between them a language will be forged leading to mutual revelation until the day when, moving from certitude to certitude—with the inevitable ups and downs—each will be convinced of sincerity of the other's love. The last stop will be taken in faith, when the sum of experiences has given such certitude that one can risk all. But this ultimate step implies a self-commitment to the other in a greater and more intense trust than any previous act. It is the perception of the heart of the person that is only given to total trust, in other words, to an act of faith.

This analysis will help us grasp the workings of religious faith. Here, in the Gospel, we have Christ offering the mystery of the divine life that man could never have imagined on his own. Christ did this simply by living it himself. And this divine life was his own life. He revealed and explained it as he lived it out before his apostles. When he wanted to share this divine life with anyone he asked them to believe in him. The rest is his affair. What he asks is that they believe him, and believe in him. That is all.

Whatever shape the calls to faith may take, in ultimate analysis, he always demands faith in himself—not in a mystery or a truth proclaimed in speculative terms, but in a concrete act of faith. "If anyone wishes to be a follower of mine he must take up his cross and come with me" (Mt 16:24). "If you wish to go the whole way, go, sell your possessions . . . and come, follow me" (Mt 19:21). He reminds those who wanted to follow him that the Son of Man had nowhere to lay his head (Mt 8:20; Lk 9:58). Faith is total trust that involves the sum total of existence, not mere adhesion to a doctrine, for this doctrine of Christ's is a life infleshed in daily life.

In the Gospel we see Jesus asking those who draw near to believe more than they see. He shows a power and wisdom far beyond what would normally be expected from a carpenter's son. And that is precisely what he wants us to believe. At the start "that" is something rather vague. After his first preaching and contacts, when anyone says "I believe," it simply means, "I believe you are a great prophet, even, maybe, the Messiah." As yet there is no question of "I believe that you are the Son of God." That will only be possible later.

The man who says "I believe" thinks he has sufficient reason to consider that Jesus is more than meets the eye. It is a first venture beyond ordinary, everyday experience, on the way to a further and different type of intellectual adhesion that also includes knowledge.

2. Progressive awakening of faith

Ordinarily, faith awakens gradually as in the case of the Samaritan woman in her long conversation with Jesus at Jacob's well. When Jesus asked her for a drink she answered: "What! You, a Jew, ask a drink of me, a Samaritan woman!" "If you only knew what God gives," Jesus replied, "and who it is that is asking you for a drink, you would have asked him and he would have given you living water" (Jn 4:9-10).

She then asked how he could give her water: "Are you greater than Jacob our ancestor, who gave us this well, and drank from it himself, he and his sons and his cattle too?" Jesus then explained the kind of water he was promising and the woman begged to have some. But when Jesus told her to fetch her husband in the town she said she had none. "You are right," Jesus answered, "in saying you have no husband, for although you have had five husbands, the man with whom you are now living is not your husband; you told me the truth there." Overcome, the Samaritan woman cried: "Sir, I can see you are a prophet" (Jn 4:11ff).

This woman has just made an act of faith. To believe in Jesus as a prophet is to recognize he is no ordinary man but has special powers and particular knowledge of the things of

God. Hence, she wanted to go on with the discussion and asked Jesus if Jews or Samaritans are right about the place where God should be adored: is it Mount Garizim in Samaria or in Jerusalem? Jesus explained that the time had come when the place will be unimportant, for "the time approaches, indeed it is already here, when those who are real worshipers will worship the Father in spirit and truth" (Jn 4:23). And the conversation goes on. Finally the Samaritan ran off to the town and told the people: "Come and see a man who has told me everything I ever did. Could this be the Messiah?" (Jn 4:29).

She was already won over to the idea that this man is no ordinary prophet, not even one of the prophets. He is unique; he is the Christ. We cannot know exactly what the woman put under the term "Christ," but it is certain that she made an act of faith in the mysterious mission of this man. The people of Sychar then invited Jesus to stay with them and he did so for two days. Many more believed because of his word, and they told the woman: "It is no longer because of what you said that we believe, for we have heard him ourselves, and we know that this is in truth the Savior of the world" (Jn 4:41-42).

There are various other roads to faith in other Gospel passages that might be analyzed. In every case we find faith in a "personality" of Christ that lies beyond the obvious. People see more or less deeply. For some, Jesus is nothing but imposter, blasphemer and hypocrite. Others see him as a man like any other. And then there are those who take him for a prophet, even maybe the Messiah. Now the word Messiah has very strong overtones among the Jews, for regarding Messiahs there is but one, for whom everyone is impatiently waiting, who will one day be the great leader of Israel.

One day Jesus put this question to his disciples: "Who do men say the Son of Man is?" They answered: "Some say John the Baptist, others Elijah, others Jeremiah, or one of the prophets." "And you," he asked, "who do you say I am?" Simon Peter answered: "You are the Messiah, the Son of the living God." Then Jesus said: "Simon, son of John, you are favored indeed! You did not learn that from mortal man; it was revealed to you by my heavenly Father" (Mt 16:13-17).

What meaning Peter gave to the expression "the Messiah, the Son of the living God," is open to discussion. But certainly Christ realized he was giving it an out-of-the-ordinary sense. "It is easy enough to call me a prophet or Elijah or Jeremiah, he seemed to say, but what you are saying of me, you could never have made up on your own by what you know of Scripture." Peter had made an authentic act of faith in the presence in Jesus of a very special personality. He could not have discovered Christ's inner nature without a particular light from the Father.

3. The mystery of the act of faith

We touch here on the mystery of the act of faith. In every way human, as we see in the case of the Samaritan woman and of Peter, this act of faith in the superior nature of Christ cannot be made without the grace of God. Ultimately, the soul often is unaware that Christ himself is enlightening it as he proposes the reality of his mystery.

Already, then, the human relationship of Christ contains a divine action that makes faith in his divinity possible and desirable. Our unwillingness to commit ourselves to the relationship would normally block the way for Christ to enlighten us about his mystery.

The initial act of confidence involves us in a relationship that means running the risk of faith. We are committed far enough in this relationship to enable God to demonstrate the certitude of our act of faith, yet we retain the possibility of withdrawing and backing out if, once we have envisaged the consequences, we are not prepared to take the risk.

This may explain what is happening as we move toward faith. For many people, though, faith seems so attractive and right that they accept the risk and believe without hesitation. From that very instant they grasp what Christ is talking about from Christ's own inner point of view. Faith is now a real knowledge, as real and even more so than any human knowing.

In short, faith has become objective knowledge, accepted as someone else's truth, a bare reality believed on another man's word, and not simply a feeling. The objective character of knowledge by faith needs to be grasped carefully. It is not primarily the outcome of experience or an impression, nor is it a projection. It is belief in Christ the Son of God on the word of men who knew him. They had to make their way painfully, and we accept as objective truth the result of their experience, trusting in them, and in so doing, trusting in Christ.

What we believe may cut across our normal thought-patterns but we accept it. Why is this? Because the way the apostles took to reach faith seems to us both wise and true—above all because acceptance of faith changed their whole lives, and this is, perhaps, the strongest of all arguments.

By the act of faith we seem to step over into another world. In the very act we have an intuition of the divine goal of the relationship, one that no longer escapes us. Certainly, we can never know God absolutely as he is, because that would make us God. Yet in a very true sense when we see him as he is, we shall be transformed into him. John says it: "We shall be like him because we shall see him as he is" (1 Jn 1:1-4).

Knowledge of God as he is is promised for another life when God will be made manifest. But even now it is offered to us in faith.

4. Faith in Christ Jesus

St. John gives us a wonderful initiation into the mysteries of faith. All through his Gospel he traces its ways and in his First Epistle he explains what faith in Christ meant for him. He saw, touched and heard a man, but what, in fact, he saw, touched and heard was the very word of God. "It was there from the beginning; we have heard it; we have seen it with our own eyes; we looked upon it, and felt it with our own hands; and it is of this we tell. Our theme is the word of life. This life was made visible, we have seen it and bear testimony; we here declare to you the eternal life which dwelt

with the Father and was made visible to us. What we have
seen and heard we declare to you, so that you and we
together may share in a common life, that life which we
share with the Father and his Son Jesus Christ. And we
write this in order that the joy of us all may be complete" (1
Jn 1:1-4).

For John, as for all those who had known Christ
intimately, what he did and said could only be explained
basically by the fact that he had a very special relationship
with God. This is what he wanted to bring here to us. In so
doing he revealed the ultimate goal of our spiritual life,
which is God. He has helped us to believe in the unbelievable,
that has become for us as true as our very existence.

The faith-process is a very complex phenomenon that
Ladislaus Boros has analyzed very deeply in *God Is With
Us*:

> The more we read and analyze what is said of Jesus,
> the more we are led to conclude that he is not merely
> a man like us. Never, in fact, has a man revealed
> such depths of being and thought. Taken as mere
> man, all our conclusions fall flat. Only an existen-
> tial analysis of his person and work will enable us to
> see him as both perfect man and absolutely other. It
> is not by trying to escape the analysis of his human
> reality but by pushing it to its extreme consequences
> that we shall see how this man was at the same time
> more than a man.

> When we come to a full stop in our philosophy of the
> person of Jesus, we are up against the altogether
> other and the ultimate depth of all reality. The effort
> and blockage of human thought—on the level of the
> concrete reality of Jesus, or, rather, through it—will
> be for us the chance of a revelation of the divine
> sphere. At the heart of our powerless efforts, we
> shall see rise up, by way of contrast, the outline of
> the inconceivable being existing outside all human

grasp. Through these fumblings we experience the existential shock that brings us into God's presence.

The author sums up briefly his aim in writing the book: "In short, the aim of the essays you will read is solely to show the failure of our human concepts to express the reality of Jesus, by demonstrating by this very fact that, thanks to this failure, Jesus appears to us as the perfect existential way to lead us to God."

Such a process brings us to the faith as described. Jesus performs deeds and above all says and reveals such things that no explanation on the human level can account for his behavior. His human activities in a world where we are at home challenge us, and that we have to face. All our stock of human realities gives us no answer, and we simply have to say that we do not know why Christ speaks and acts as he does. We cannot explain "him." This is where we have to risk trusting his words if we are to understand him, listening humbly to his own explanation of himself. It is the certainty that this man is like no other, but a being who draws me away beyond the level of human explanations to the risk of the act of faith. This is how we come to the notion of a spiritual life consisting of attention to the mystery of Christ, mystery of God.

5. How to live the inner life of faith

When we make an act of faith in Jesus Christ we believe him on his word and reach a new mode of knowing. That he is good, says things no one else has said and opens up infinite horizons, we know. This direct knowledge of Christ makes us believe him incapable of deceiving us and prepares us to believe his teaching. To the Samaritan he says: "If only you knew what God gives and who it is that is asking you for a drink" (Jn 4:10). Soon this woman will be ready to believe anything.

What happens after we say "I believe" to Christ? Apparently nothing spectacular. Yet something has changed. We have stepped into a new inner world revealed by Christ. God has become for us the Father who makes us his children. We call ourselves children of God and so we really are, as John says in his First Epistle (1 Jn 3:1). As we follow Christ's words we come upon God's amazing inner world where there is a Father who is Christ's Father, a Spirit who is the Spirit of the Father and the Son. Christ gives no catechism answer to this definition of the mystery. He simply alerts us to its implications in his own life and ours.

Since all this is shrouded in mystery, we can only come back again and again to the original texts of Christ's first revelation. There we stay, reverencing the mystery, striving to read what we are able to grasp of the reality Christ places before us. But for each flash of intuition there is a gulf of mystery. With what we have managed to perceive we gain strength to remain silent in face of the incomprehensible.

At this point in our faith-process we can say we have left behind the common ways of human knowledge. Not that knowledge of faith is inhuman, but it is an invitation to a super-human mode of knowing. This is perfectly understandable. The object of faith being the mystery of God, only God can speak of God and make himself known.

As long as created realities alone are the objects of our experience and thought, our knowing capacity expands only to deal with what is before it. Our knowing and loving faculties work in a so-called normal mode. But our spirit has faculties that are deeper—not different, but underdeveloped potentialities within those we possess already. When Christ comes proposing a mystery that is neither abstract nor purely intellectual, our knowing capacities will expand and deepen. If then we believe what Christ says, a mysterious communication will arise between us. He is enabling us to believe in his teaching in the most natural way in the world. We can now know with greater depth and breadth. Before that, we were unaware that we could grasp the vastness of the mystery, even without understanding the whole; suddenly, under Christ's influence, our hidden possibilities of understanding and living lie open before us (Eph 3:14-21).

To adhere to Christ in an act of faith leads us to a twofold discovery—the depth of God and the depth of man. When we reach this mode of knowing we may have a sudden, swift intuition of the infinite inner space that faith could one day unveil. The field of faith-knowledge is as immense as God himself. Yet it does not disturb us, knowing as we do that it is a knowledge "within" Christ in whom we discover the divine mystery.

In practice, we always have to come back to our certainty of Christ. The act of faith is an extraordinary risk. Man becomes involved in an adventure of which he does not see the end—hence the need to rely continually on Christ and what he tells us in the Gospel. It contains all Christ had to say, but we shall never understand that perfectly, because it is not a question of grasping maxims and definitions but contact with a living reality we call God. Faith tends not to knowledge but to life, and that is why it must become experience. To say that faith must become experience means that belief must be integrated into human experience. No doubt, the object of faith is revealed to us by Christ, and without God's grace we cannot attain this knowledge, but finally it has to become our own. It has, therefore, to enter necessarily the normal field of our knowing activity. No other faculties than our very own, refined and deepened through grace, can lead us to a faith experience.

This is no day's work precisely because the mode remains human. The global perception of the mystery of the first act of faith is simply "believed" in an act of faith in the Church and in Christ. We accept the whole thing as it stands. It was Paul's experience on the way to Damascus. In accepting Christ he accepted everything. But years had to pass before he really grasped what this act of faith implied. Three days were spent in Damascus fasting; then there were years of retreat in Arabia followed by three or four years of reflection, and finally the great years of apostolate that led him to penetrate the depths of what he had believed at Damascus, or, more precisely, the depths of the one in whom he had believed, Christ.

In this experience we have Paul's silent acceptance of
faith, his reflection on its contents and his discovery of its
depth as he proposes it to non-Christians—above all in the
communities he founded. At the end of his life he could say:
"I know in whom I have believed" (2 Tim 1:12)—that is, he
had made no mistake in believing in Christ, and he had
discovered the one in whom he had believed. He had had an
entire lifetime to explore the contents and consequences of
an act of faith that might seem irrational, but was ultimately
justified in its confirmation through experience.

6. The Holy Spirit and the experience of faith

This experience of faith is made in the light and under
the guidance of the Holy Spirit, so we have to try to
understand his role. Christ came to "tell" us about God and
to express him in his life. But human language that would be
capable of telling about God is in itself inconceivable. Yet
Christ is the expression of God and he has explained God in
human terms. Here are the words that express a life, and
they exist in order to reveal God. The true meaning of these
words can only be understood when we are inwardly
enlightened. The Word of God is there before us as an object
of knowledge, but he is within us too, to illuminate what has
been said, God stands in Christ as language and at the same
time in us as interpreter of the language. And this
explanation is given by the Holy Spirit in whose light we are
enabled to understand and penetrate the true meaning of
Christ's message.

When Christ promised the coming of the Spirit he
explained his role. It would be first a helping role: the
Paraclete would help the disciples to triumph in the great
conflict that would set them against the world. On the other
hand, his action would be essentially inward and he would
act as the spirit of truth; his role there would be to strengthen
the disciples' faith in Jesus.

These two activities of the Spirit, in fact, tend toward the
same end. He has to protect the disciples in their struggle

against the world. Christ did not mean he would shield them from persecution but that he would give them strength to say what they should say and the courage to bear witness to his truth and his message. In the face of earthly judges, the Holy Spirit would give them the strength to proclaim the existence of the world of faith. This is very clear in our days—an affirmation that this world is fulfilled neither in itself nor for itself but that it opens onto the world of faith that Christ came to reveal. Since this stand cannot be taken without divine light, Christ has promised the assistance of the Holy Spirit for the trial of the disciples' faith. There is no need, then, for anxiety as to what to say; the words will be provided by the Spirit.

Further, the Holy Spirit has the protective role of Paraclete to shelter the disciples against the milieu of the world—the unbelieving world, that is, which thinks it is all in all and that everything revolves around it. This seduction of human thought is growing always more powerful; hence the need to be ceaselessly attentive to what the Holy Spirit inspires to make us comprehend the truth and grandeur of the faith.

The Holy Spirit acts within the heart. Uttering no words; he simply illumines the words of Jesus, giving a meaning to his revelation of God. The Spirit's role is one of teaching, but from within. After saying many things to his disciples, Jesus concludes: "I have told you all this while I am still here with you; but your Advocate, the Holy Spirit whom the Father will send in my name, will teach you everything, and will call to mind all that I have told you" (Jn 14:25-26). Christ's role as incarnate Word has been to speak of God to us. The role of the Holy Spirit is to give meaning to this language by helping us to grasp its relationship with the divine reality it expresses.

The Holy Spirit, then, has no revelation of his own apart from Jesus. When Jesus says that the Spirit will teach the disciples he does not imply anything new. The role of the Spirit is essentially subordinate to the revelation brought by Christ. The world "teach" in St. John is almost a revelation-word. The Father has taught the Son what he himself has communicated to the world (Jn 8:28). Christ's doctrine, however, must not remain outside the believer; John insists strongly on the need to interiorize it by ever-growing living faith. This is the meaning of the typically Johannine expressions: "Dwell with the doctrine of Christ" (2 Jn 9), "Dwell within the revelation-word" (Jn 8:31; 15:7-8). This is precisely where the action of the Spirit takes place; he also teaches—teaches what has already been said by Jesus so that it penetrates hearts. Thus there is perfect continuity of revelation: issuing from the Father, it is communicated by the Son and reaches its term only when it has penetrated to our innermost selves through the action of the Spirit.

Our Lord also told the disciples that the Spirit would call to mind all that he had told them. This was not a mere reminder of truths in case the disciples should forget them. His true task would be to give them an inner understanding of Christ's words so as to grasp them in the light of faith and penetrate all their virtues and wealth for the life of the Church. The secret action of the Spirit causes Jesus' message to cease being exterior and foreign to us; he interiorizes it and helps us to penetrate it spiritually to discover the Word of Life. This is what John in his First Epistle calls the "anointing" that dwells in us (1 Jn 2:27); the teaching of Jesus in the heart of the believer gives him an inner sense of truth (1 Jn 2:20-21) and instructs him about everything; henceforth, the Christian is born of the Spirit (Jn 3:8). Having reached this degree of spiritual maturity he no longer needs teaching (1 Jn 2:27); he has only to remain with Jesus and let himself be taught by God (Jn 6:45).

These texts help us to a better understanding of how spiritual experience in faith comes about. Christ has revealed the Father and we have accepted this revelation in faith. But without the very light of God brought by the Spirit we cannot understand the words of Jesus or their profound significance. Even this light can only be accepted and grasped in faith. At times we may perceive the unction of the Spirit in us in a mysterious but very real way, but not always.

7. Continual attention in faith

Normally, the Holy Spirit only gives inward teaching to those who, believing firmly in his action, listen with the "ear of their heart" to his words. We may only seek to hear him in faith, and it is in faith that we hear and understand him. Given this disposition of total faith, all Christ said takes on astounding relevance. Everything appears true. It is no longer the belief of the first day we met when our act of faith still seemed a risk to be run, and run freely. Now, lit up from within, we see these truths with a clarity that demands our adhesion. This is the result of the action of the Spirit. Inwardly enlightened by him, this same light illumines what we believe.

In the words of the Buddhists, we have now "reached the other shore." They speak of nirvana in these terms. For us this simply means: We started out on our pilgrimage on this shore, judging everything from a human point of view. After seeing and hearing Christ we took the risk of believing him. Through periods of uncertainty we tried to understand what we had accepted to believe. We listened to our inner self, trying to hear the one who was to explain everything. Without quite knowing how, as we read and reread the Gospel texts, pondering the words of Jesus, we became aware of a growing conviction and light. Already we were no longer on the shore we had left behind us long ago. Evangelical truths now appeared bathed in a different light than that of human intelligence; they were already immersed in the divine light. Then one day it seemed to us that we set foot on a new earth, God's land. Without leaving the world of men we were now capable of grasping divine truths in the light of God. We were grounded in the faith.

For a man who has come this far, faith is its own justification. But to reach this kind of understanding we must have set foot on the further shore. We must have accepted Christ wholly.

How can this experience of faith be lived in the concrete? There are a variety of methods suiting different persons, though the attitudes and essential steps are identical. We shall speak of this later. However, all are characterized by mindfulness of the mystery of the divine life in us. This divine life that is to transform us is normally hidden and breaks into our experience on a different level from our other inner, intellectual activities; but we should be acting and living in such a way that we are always ready to allow the divine life to influence our actions.

Practically speaking, the easiest way to pray and meditate is to take up an attitude of respectful waiting for the divine light. We can read the Gospel and ponder as much as possible to get at its meaning. But we know very well that these texts are as deep as the one who inspired them. Hence, while striving to penetrate the Gospel truths, we should always be aware of a teaching and light that come from the depths of our heart. Making efforts, we maintain a humble conviction that truths of faith can only be understood in the light of God. Such a humble and confident attitude of ours is an appeal that God sees very well. He responds through the action of the Holy Spirit who brings us understanding and a taste of what we have the joy to believe.

8. Faith and the so-called charismatic action of the Spirit

A great deal more remains to be said about faith, but we shall deal with it in connection with other problems of the spiritual life. What has been said so far is enough to show that this life is a life in faith, and at the same time to give a glimpse of how it may be lived. It is the great mystery that those alone penetrate who are willing to give themselves up totally to the action of Christ and the Spirit to reach the knowledge of the love of the Father. All this may leave those who belong to pentecostal or charismatic movements dissatisfied. As they read these lines they will say that we have left out the Spirit's action in the Church of our times. The Spirit, they will say, acts not only in discreet and hidden modes but in broad daylight and even violently. No doubt the Spirit does act in this way; nevertheless, faith remains basic, and what people call "experience" may never be allowed to set faith to one side. Faith is the final norm of experience because what commonly goes by the name of experience must itself be submitted to discernment in the light of faith. This will always be so until we see God face to face.

What is required by prayer according to the Spirit is belief in the presence and action of God in us through the power of his Spirit. As in the early Church, this may be manifested by marvelous gifts such as "glossolalia" or speaking in tongues. The person who prays in this way is bidden to let the Spirit pray in him and give himself up to his action. Such an initial act of faith is destined to remove voluntary or involuntary obstacles. Thus there must be trust in the Spirit, listening and even letting him move us by accepting the loss of a certain amount of self-control. Given all this, what is commonly known as speaking in tongues is easily explicable. The motion of the Spirit, whose source is at greater depth than our sub-conscious, becomes a language that flows like water from its source. This is the charism. There may perhaps be imitations, when speaking in tongues does not express a specific action of the Spirit but a way of praying conditioned by the atmosphere of the assembly. The discernment problem that then arises will be dealt with at the end of Chapter VI.

Those who receive what is called baptism in the Spirit undoubtedly enjoy a marvelous experience. What they believed in naked faith is now direct experience. God lives in them and loves them, just as if suddenly the Spirit, hidden up to then, had sprung up and manifested himself. These persons live in God and God in them, like truly newborn beings in the power of the Spirit. Their faith has become luminous, their joy overflowing. It is a baptism where they are plunged into an enfolding light and love. All is new, all is clear, all is joy in them and around them.

To those who have received this grace faith may seem less necessary when the evidence is so overwhelming. But whatever its strength, the experience is always based on faith. Ultimately it is only in faith that I perceive the whole depth of this experience which gives it its final dimension.

Delusions are always possible, and we may take our imaginations for special communications from God. No one is safe from such mishaps. Thus we have always to come back to the faith whose doors have been opened to us by the Word of God. Christ meant this when he said of the Spirit: "The Paraclete, the Holy Spirit whom the Father will send in my name, will teach you everything, and will call to mind all that I have told you" (Jn 14:26).

He says nothing new because the Word is the Father's total revelation. He says nothing of himself, and we have always to come back to the light the incarnate Word left us that the Spirit helps us to receive and understand.

Even at the very heart of the experience, faith must be there, living and acting. It can save us from illusions and lead us past emotional fascination. Through faith we go beyond the signs of the divine action to grasp it in its very essence. Never can the importance of faith be too much emphasized at a time when there exists such powerful craving for spiritual experiences. Faith alone can keep us from error; only faith can lead us on ceaselessly toward an ever deeper meeting with the living God, dwelling in inaccessible light, in which alone he can be seen.

III

Discovery of the Spiritual Meaning of Existence

The spiritual life is not lived on some other planet. Mindfulness of God in faith, which is the very essence of this spiritual life, is based on the reality of our essential humanity and within our concrete existence. Like Christ, therefore, our spiritual life is human in the strictest sense of the word, while, at the same time, divine. Maybe we could call it supernatural if many people did not object to a word that seems to be contrary to natural. In the present case the word "divine" signifies more than supernatural, and it has this advantage: it does not accentuate opposition to the natural.

Whether we like it or not, we do not relinquish our humanity to reach God, yet we come to a knowledge so much beyond us that we can attain it only in joint action with God. How can this happen? Participation is the only word we have to explain this fact, and only those who have arrived at this knowledge of God can understand it. In these matters definitions tell us nothing; experience says everything. What is out of reach of analysis we find in concrete action. If we never commit ourselves to live a spiritual life, being content with mere discussion, we are like someone who is forever talking about the art of the violin without ever actually getting down to playing it.

This principle should also be understood in a wider sense. The spiritual life is not an intellectual exercise, a meditation or contemplation, but total, essential attention. When something absorbs us, our whole attention is concentrated and even our body is carried away, like the branches of a tree caught up in a typhoon that seem to flow like waters of a wild torrent overflowing its banks. If they could, these branches would fly away with the wind but they are held back by the trunk.

Allured by a mysterious presence we are drawn out of ourselves. If we could we would leave this worldly existence to lose ourselves in God. The same happens in self-discovery when we enter a beyond that captivates our attention and finally enraptures us.

1. Discovery of God in Scripture

Were I speaking to non-Christians I would not start out by the discovery of God in Holy Scripture, but with human psychology. I would try to lead them along the road taken by so many men as they set out to find God. However, when we deal with non-believers, this path, though necessary, is somewhat lengthy. Besides, in traveling along this road we come to the obstacles that all religious geniuses have met, chief among which is the difficulty of finding God. In this respect Buddha is a characteristic example. He solved the problem by simply refusing to speak of God to his disciples.

But for us the way to God is wide open, already there in Scripture. It needs to be made practicable and broadened in every direction. I have chosen to take the road Christ outlined for me, one he knows well because the way is himself. As I go forward I shall realize how wisely I have chosen.

The inner life is mindfulness or attention to God. But when God inspired Holy Scripture it was to set ground-lights along his way through human history.

The outlook of Scripture is very different from that of the early Buddhist writings. It introduces us to a knowledge of God that Buddha refused to transmit because he said such knowledge was useless. The consequences of this attitude have had grave repercussions on Buddhism whose wise men, nevertheless, have tried to get to the heart of the mystery Buddha refused to discuss.

Scripture is God's Word to mankind. The mystery of God is not manifested from the viewpoint of someone like Buddha, who would make superhuman efforts to reach it, but from that of a Being dominating all things—the history of the world and the divine itself. Hence, we attribute the inspiration of Scripture to the Spirit who knows the secrets of God and man. As we read we feel as if the one who inspired it holds the story of the universe and mankind in the palm of his hand, from the day before all days when God created the world until the day described in the Book of Revelation when all things will return to God.

We should have a humble attitude toward Holy Scripture, like someone receiving a revelation of God's action and being. Christ himself, in whom we have believed, brings it to us, and through it God's speech becomes ever more explicit. As the Letter to the Hebrews says: "When in former times God spoke to our forefathers, he spoke in a fragmentary and varied fashion through the prophets. But in this final age he has spoken to us by the Son whom he has made heir to the whole universe, and through whom he created all orders of existence" (Heb 1:1-2).

God began by making himself known in a vague way through the prophets and the great Old Testament patriarchs, but he kept the revelation of his inner life for his only Son. If the saints of the Old Law could already open up immense horizons on God, only the Son could tell us what God is. As St. John says, "No one has ever seen God; but God's only Son, he who is nearest to the Father's heart, he has made him known" (Jn 1:18).

The Old Testament leads us to recognize God among all the man-made divinities, and to discover his way in human history. God is manifested by Christ, his Son, in the Gospels. The Acts of the Apostles and the Epistles plunge us back into concrete reality, but a reality illumined by the presence and knowledge of Christ living in history.

2. The concrete light of Scripture

In practice, Scripture reading should have a very special place in the lives of those who aspire to an inner life. It is precisely in the Bible that we perceive the interior aspect of human things in a divine perspective, and it is there that we discover the great truths. By repeated reading of Scripture texts these truths become the beacons of our whole existence.

We do not need profound Scripture studies to profit by our reading, but we should have sufficient knowledge of the cultural milieu that will enable us to grasp what the sacred writer is trying to convey. And once we have this it is only a question of trying to get at the value of the teaching that the Lord wants to give us.

The Book of Genesis opens with a fundamental statement: God is the one who bestows life and consciousness. God alone, then, is wholly active; he it is who has the initiative. The Bible as a whole is filled with the idea that all comes from God's hands and everything is the work of his wisdom. Man has received his life from God, a fact that in no way contradicts evolution which only starts after creation. There was a time when nothing existed but God. "In the beginning God created heaven and earth" (Gen 1:1). John alludes to this creation in the first chapter of his Gospel: "When all things began, the Word already was. The Word dwelt with God, and what God was, the Word was. The Word, then, was with God at the beginning, and through him all things came to be; no single thing was created without him" (Jn 1:1-2).

These and many other texts that introduce us to our basic relationship with God should awaken in us an inner, deep and overwhelming sense of the link uniting us with our Creator. The thought should be with us all through life to give it its correct perspective in relation to the Absolute. At this point there is no more need to prove to ourselves that God exists, but rather a need to attain a vital certitude that will express our intellectual conviction in human terms. If those thoughts become familiar to us our life as a whole will seem wholly linked with the divine act that made the world exist.

Such a mental conviction has to become an intellectual, affective, and rooted certitude.

Similarly, we can explore Scripture to try to grasp the meaning of human liberty. This should be done on the same grounds as our discovery of dependence. We shall then find out an astounding fact: God has made man so much his image that he has made him free, and, before all, free in regard to God himself. All other possibilities of freedom are relative, but this one is fundamental: man is able to stand up against God.

This truth is affirmed in the account of Adam's sin and taken up again in other sacred books. It is a truth I live and can discern running through my whole existence. Adam's sin becomes comprehensible when we look into our own hearts, at our doorstep. When we reflect on it we cannot relegate it to a distant past, for in it we acknowledge our own sin: Adam's sin is ours. It is a sin we understand, every man's sin and so our own; we were there, tempted in Adam like all other men. This is the way that Scripture leads us to recognize our personal responsibility before God; when we refuse him what he wants we are shrinking from his gaze.

In meditation or contemplation no more distance remains between my daily life and the fact as related in the Bible, because Scripture has been written to be for me an ever-present light. As an account of past events it is history, but the divine intention is to reach me in whatever age I may happen to live. All mankind files before its pages, and each of its episodes is placed in a light that is God's judgment on the actions of men.

3. Human history in the light of Scripture

My whole life should be checked on God's teaching communicated to me in Scripture. It is normal that I should be moved, troubled and challenged by the text, and it would be surprising were it otherwise. Nonetheless, there does exist a certain way of meditating, contemplating and pondering Scripture that makes the truths that should rouse us completely innocuous.

If this applies to us it simply means that meditation and contemplation are mere academic exercises on unimportant problems and not really encounters of our whole selves, body, soul and heart, with the One who comes to meet us in Scripture. For that is what it is all about: God coming there to meet us, whether through human history, poetry or the prophetic warnings.

Since familiarity with Scripture is meant to provoke an encounter, we need to be very wide awake when we start to read. But how many people meditate and contemplate absent-mindedly!

Every human situation passes before our eyes in the Bible, every variety of temptation and sin, of the spirit or the flesh, from Adam's temptation to that of the Israelites in the desert and Susanna's in her husband's garden. There we meet humanity in the raw, made of the same stuff as ourselves, but from the narrative emerges also a lesson which is the divine light shed on what is happening.

When Confucius composed the *Ch'un-ch'iu, Annals of Spring and Autumn,* he used the story he was telling to pass judgment on persons and things. These judgments were based on profound human wisdom which gave the wise man a penetrating insight into events. Confucius thought that when the Chinese read his book they would be able to find enough light to guide them, whether they were kings, princes or simple citizens. It was history written as a mirror for future generations. In Chinese thought the mirror concept of history is basic: it should be a mirror to govern by, and, in fact, this is the title of the important work of *Szu-ma Kuang,* the *Tzu-chih t'ung chien* or *Universal Mirror for Government.*

In China, history provides rules for behavior. This existential philosophy has had greater influence in the formation of the Chinese mentality than the philosophy itself, because the Chinese have a strong feeling for history and those who make it. Their culture is a history, which explains why it can less readily take on a truly universal dimension as compared with intellectual Western culture. The historical wisdom drawn by the erudite and cultured classes from history is what these same people and the masses drew from famous historical romances and the theater which reproduced its main episodes. These stories, romances and plays contain a vast human wisdom that has been the inspiration of Chinese culture.

Beyond its human perspectives, Holy Scripture links our history with superhuman norms. Like the human being, history has a supra- or meta-historical repercussion. It is the mystery of our history that it is both human and earthly yet tends toward another form of existence. Scripture wants to direct our thoughts toward this other mode of being while giving us norms by which to judge worldly values in view of future ones. Since these norms of judgment and action lie beyond human moral values, we have to receive them as revelation. Our whole problem is that to grasp them we have to accept them on faith. In front of us lies a superhuman wisdom that can only be understood when we humbly accept the divine light.

This is anything but passive acceptance. We have to be involved with all our capacities for knowing, which is what authentic meditation on Holy Scripture really is. We try to place ourselves under its light and let it strip us, with our strong and weak points, for our total existence has to be tested by the Bible.

This existential confrontation ultimately puts me face to face with God himself, in such a way that I get to know him, not as a distant figure but as the very source of my being and the final judge of my existence.

God tried to teach the Jewish people this throughout their history, and so he always needed witnesses. Abraham's vocation was to be the first confessor of the faith. He believed that the history of the world possessed a deeper meaning than was apparent on the surface. Gradually, but not all at once, the significance of his own past dawned on him. There had to be successive revelations in which the very life of Abraham and his family was menaced. But this was the way he learned to understand God's interventions in a human life.

Because he believed in God's work, Abraham performed some extremely important acts, and life itself confirmed his faith. He realized that he had done well to place himself in

God's hands. We like to reverse the process and have the proofs before acting. But faith is anterior to any concrete proofs we could draw from the success of anything we have undertaken in its light. This is what the risk of faith really is. And Abraham took it and became the father of all believers.

Before describing the exemplary faith of the ancients— Abel, Noah and especially Abraham and the patriarchs— the author of the Letter to the Hebrews explains the primary role of faith in human existence: "By faith we perceive that the universe was fashioned by the word of God so that the visible came forth from the invisible" (Heb 11:3).

4. The Christian as witness to God in marriage and celibacy

There is a spiritual sense in our own story just as there is to the history of Israel and human history in general. The revelation of the spiritual meaning of history gives it a fresh, depth dimension, at the same time leaving it fully human. This might be called a tension toward the beyond, an aspiration for spiritual survival and an affirmation of the truth that "I am born of the spirit."

The supreme witness of this spiritual dimension of existence is Christ, the perfect image of the Father. But after him, millions of Christians in union with the faithful of other religions have to bring their testimony to bear on these same spiritual realities.

For an adult, the normal state of life is marriage. God created man male and female, and neither the one nor the other is made to be alone. Man and woman are created to unite their lives in one single existence. It is not enough to unite occasionally to produce children. They are drawn to one another by a powerful attraction that finds intense satisfaction in intimate union; but fleshly union alone is unable to fulfill the desires for fusion of two beings who love each other. This may explain why the intimacies marriage supposes—even sexual union itself—are only a part, important but limited, of the intimacy of love.

Such desire of fusion is no mere instinct but the very fruit and expression of love. Above all it is a means of realizing a deeper union still. When the sexual desire has been satisfied, there yet remains a longing for union which is the call of the spirit.

As long as total communion of heart and spirit is not reached, union is not attained, and this demonstrates the spiritual value of relationship between the two sexes. The attraction of desire is a fruit of the Spirit who put men into existence creating them male and female. Total union is only reached finally in and through the power of the Spirit. If those who attain the heights of love contemplate this love of theirs, they cannot fail to recognize its divine origin when they see it so far beyond them.

By actualizing this mystery of their own life, Christians in their human condition become witnesses to the divine presence and action in the world. There are still, however, some men and women who know they are called to renounce marriage. If this is so, is it not because they are to express in their lives precisely that love which married people perceive at the depth and above their own love? Divine love draws these men and women to a relationship far different from the love of husband and wife. Called celibacy, a man truly witnesses to this "other" love which married couples perceive at the essence of their mutual love.

It follows that if marriage is man's "normal" and ordinary road, celibacy is not for that reason "abnormal." As compared with marriage, celibacy calls to another, more radical form of relationship with God, and if it attains a particular quality it is because such a love is lived wholly in faith. We can neither see nor touch the one we love, but the celibate knows that there is in his life a love-encounter that far outstrips any other love.

The main element of consecrated celibacy is not renouncement, but the sign value of the reality of the kingdom of God and the possibility it gives for a type of relationship with God not so easily developed in marriage. Celibacy, then, becomes the normal condition for a more vertical, immediate relationship with God, more direct than

in marriage. Unless we admit this possibility, it would have
no meaning, and then marriage alone would enable us to
respond to God's love. But should a man feel called to vow a
love that overleaps conjugal relationship, then celibacy is
significant. It senses such love of God that only a total gift
excluding conjugal love can be the answer. But this by no
means forbids other forms of love; quite the contrary is true.

Celibacy is, then, first and foremost a sign of an
inexpressible response to an unutterable love, and it is of the
same order as the approach to God by the "negative" way.
To give God a name is to claim to know him positively; but to
know he can be given no name and to approach him by the
"negative" way is to know him much better. To renounce
giving the human expression, usual in our condition, to our
response to love is to recognize that it is divine. This human
face of love will be given by those who marry, but anyone
who has experienced God in the way we have described
cannot find the answer to God's offer of love in the conjugal
life. Thus he chooses celibacy, which means that he has
penetrated the inexpressible character of this love. Great
inner solitude will always be his because he has refused to let
human love prevent him from responding to the call of love.
He is well aware that married people may love God as much
and even more than he, but for him celibacy is the only way.
Why? Finally for the inexplicable reason that this is how he
sees his response to the demands of love. Then this love
attained through renunciation, and apparently negative at
first sight, is now manifested in all its positiveness: an
immense love seeking unlimited space.

Another meaning of celibacy must be mentioned here.
Many people like to think of it as a sign of the future human
condition in the next life when what is of the flesh will have
disappeared. Even now there must be some precursors of this
future of man. Such lives are a sign of the age to come. But
this eschatological aspect, to be understood aright, should be
interpreted in the light of what has been said above.
Marriage itself, as much as celibacy, is a sign of the age to
come (Rev 21).

In Christianity, celibacy for the kingdom has always held deep significance, for it affirms a unique relationship between a man and his God. To discuss the personal reasons of those who are attached to God in this way is as difficult as if we were to ask explanations of Abraham, Paul and a multitude of others. In the end it remains true that celibacy is a radical sign of the absoluteness of a love relationship with God, to be accepted as such whether or not the reasons are immediately apparent to us.

5. God's plan and man's liberty

We should not imagine that God has a ready-made plan hidden away that we absolutely have to find out. If he has any plan, it is that he loves us, like a father who has a plan for his son and wants to work it out with him. We have to retain our liberty, and the use of that liberty is itself part of God's plan, so that we can say that our will is always enclosed in the concrete will of God.

Therefore, we have not merely to seek to know God's plan but also to accord with it, setting ourselves, mind and will, to work it out and bring it to fruition. Clearly, then, we can understand that we share with God the responsibility of our whole life.

Obviously, complete conformity of will is what matters. Thus we do not have to try to carry out blindly some ready-made plan but to strive for such union of mind and heart that we shall always be practically certain not to deviate from the divine will. By doing this we should reach that state of perfection described by Confucius in which a man could follow his deepest desires and still never step aside from perfect virtue.

This is where the spiritual life must lead us. Mindfulness of God should detach us from excessively self-centered desires to put us in line with God's will as he holds all human history in his hands. Here again we see our place in the context of cosmic history. The spiritual life leads us to try to fit in, not with passing desires that tomorrow will vanish, but with the Spirit himself who put the world into existence and animates it without end.

Christ came to reveal the final basis of our existence, that is, frames of reference and judgments not clearly seen by human intelligence when left to itself. These do not do away with our ordinary landmarks. For instance, we can localize a place by referring to familiar neighboring towns: this place is so many miles from that, and another and another, etc. Like this we can map out any position with the greatest exactitude. But more knowledgeable people will provide longitude and latitude which will be still more exact, though the man in the street will be none the wiser, because who knows where meridians and parallels are anyway? By referring to the stars experts will use a more precise system again, but no one thinks of making daily use of it.

So it is with the spiritual life which provides a framework for our life as a whole and all its activities in particular, unknown to those without faith. We learn of it through Christ's revelation and we are ready to live our life in harmony with it. This is precisely what the life of faith is all about.

6. Discernment of God's ways

Now we come to practical politics. To set out to develop a spiritual life means that we have somehow grasped that the basic pointers of our existence were in God in Christ. As we tried to understand what spiritual context was ours, we discovered the life of grace and God's indwelling in our soul as well as the immensity of divine love. Then we saw emerging out of our most humdrum daily life the presence of a deeper life that was both our own and God's.

But we also began to understand that the discovery of these spiritual elements in our lives were not given merely as objects of knowledge to contemplate. There has also been a felt call to live in greater conformity with Christ in whom we perceived the perfection of the spiritual life.

We saw Christ as the ideal, but how can we live this ideal in daily life? This is the point. It is so easy to chase after illusions and utopias with their inevitable train of failures, so if we are to respond to his love, we have to interpret the signs of God's desires.

The problem of Holy Scripture as a guide to the ways of God in this world has to be faced. A habit of meditating on the Bible with this in mind will help us to grasp God's ways of acting in the world, the history of the whole human race and our own private individual history as well.

There is a gradual entering into God's ways with us, how he treats us and how he shows us his will. There are precepts given to us by the Church in the name of Christ, and these are no great problem. The difficulty arises when we have to find out how to orientate our lives, and, that done, how we are to remain in total conformity with God.

There are a number of possibilities. At times, God's desires are shown so clearly and with such force that there is no room for doubt. This kind of light brings with it the grace of inner transformation, as was the case with Paul. The light carries its own marks of authenticity: the intensity of its brilliance and the strength that comes with it.

But matters are not always so clear-cut. Often there is neither sudden inspiration nor blinding light. More than in the first case we have to rely on experience. Decisions should now only be taken after long reflection. The pros and cons should be weighed in the light of Christ's teachings, the person's capacities and experience. Discernment takes much longer but is less risky insofar as the control is more sustained and detailed.

In instances of this kind God leaves us to reflect as we would over any other personal affair. But his light is always there as an inner help without our knowing how, guiding us to take decisions in accord with his desires. We might imagine, but wrongly, that we have been left on our own, but, unseen by us, the Spirit of God is there to help us with his presence and action. By him we discern the signs of the divine will and take decisions that will be blessed by God.

Nothing, however, replaces experience, and discernment skill needs a long learning process. There has to be time, patience, and, above all, total sincerity. Humble people are quick to acquire it because, without scrupulosity or fear, they are ready to doubt their own views.

Attention to God's signs in our lives should be neither tense nor anxious, but it must be constant. Our own life-history will provide the key to the divine action in our regard. God, in fact, has his own personal way of dealing with each one of us which we have to learn gradually. No special studies are needed, but only attention to God's ways in our life and history. Sacred history goes on revealing God to those who are ready to seek out his footsteps in their own life story.

IV

Relationship with God, Relationship with Men

Having shown the spiritual meaning of existence we have now to take a look at one of the outstanding problems of our days, expressed in such slogans as: "Relationship with God is nonsense because no one has ever seen God," or "Relationship with God is found in relationship with others," or, again, "I can only find God in others."

Because of these fairly widespread ideas, many people will no longer pray alone; they only do so in a group. Others give up all personal prayer and throw themselves into action or multiply contacts with others.

What has been said in previous chapters already answers many aspects of this problem. We want to show here that in Christian tradition man meets his neighbor as soon as he recollects himself in Christ for a moment. To set in silent opposition to the silent search for God and meeting him in human relationships is an over-simplification.

Every spiritual doctrine teaches the importance of the inner gaze that turns from outward objects to enter the heart. In a very beautiful passage St. Augustine tells how he searched for God outside himself for a long time in vain while all the time he was in the depth of his heart. Teresa of Avila repeated the same thing, as do all the great spiritual masters of all times and all religions. It was taught by

Mencius (Meng-tzu) when he told men to go to the bottom of
their hearts, and Eui-neng, the sixth Ch'an patriarch, said,
"Only by turning toward your heart can you reach
illumination, so why wear yourself out searching for it
outside?"

Spiritual men of all ages call on man to turn inward to
find their ultimate depth. Scientists run up against obstacles
in their research that mark ultimate boundaries. But the
inner dimension of the spirit is the entry to the infinite, the
door to the divine mystery.

1. Take time to be mindful of the mystery

We should give some time daily to this inner dimension.
Philosophers do this to meditate, lovers to enjoy their love.
In the same way we should take time to ponder on the divine
mystery.

Some think they do not need to give time to this
attention. There are certainly more people than we think
who have a profound view of the mystery permeating their
whole life, but it is the result of a long period of training, and
the continuing presence only came to them after a
considerable time spent in plumbing its depths.

There are others, again, who think it superfluous to turn
inward to try to reach direct relationship with God. They
claim that the road to God passes by the way of man, and so
refuse to dedicate needed attention and time to the divine
mystery. Certainly many have gone astray along this inner
path and have become introverted. To quote a French writer,
Claudel, "They think they love God because they love no
one." But this is a danger easily avoided, since an authentic
inward path is also an outward one, and when we have truly
met Christ then we turn to our neighbor.

If anyone has understood with Paul "the breadth,
length, and height and depth," he has also understood "the
love of Christ that is beyond knowledge" and has entered
through "his fullness into the fullness of God himself" (Eph
3:18-19). Expanding in every direction, at the same time he
communicates with all men by knowledge and love.

The danger for anyone rejecting attention to the mystery of God is that he will be caught up in a series of superficial relationships. Living outside himself, he will live outside other men too.

Many people find time to do an hour's yoga to gain peace and self-control; others take time off to go into abstruse problems calling for calm, quiet and silent reflection. If we are convinced there is a hidden, inner dimension to our existence we shall easily find time to try to explore it.

We know what this secret dimension is since Christ came to tell us about it. It is at the same time the divine presence within created things and infinite openness to God. Christ showed us that for him it meant a son's relationship with his Father. As man, often, perhaps every day, he took time to advert to this relationship. Leaving his disciples behind, he went off to a quiet corner and there, as man, he lived with all possible intensity his eternal relationship with the Father.

He was son, and he never lost sight of the fact; yet, being man, he had to give "time" to the human expression of this relationship. We might say that as man he needed to integrate it into his human psychology. Why not? One of the great mysteries of the life of Christ is that what he had always been he had to become in his humanity—not merely to teach us, but because he was a true man and his divinity was expressed historically in his humanity.

2. Mindfulness of God in the Christian life

For most Christians this relationship with God is expressed through ordinary Christian life: assistance at Mass, participation in the sacraments, personal prayer and practice of virtues in imitation of Christ. These forms of spiritual life practiced by Christians are their way of paying attention to the divine mystery. It is common knowledge that this may lead to a certain formalism, but what human society is without it? Some structure is needed in any life, and it would be cloud gathering to suppose otherwise.

Those who think they can keep their faith in God without ever expressing it are in great danger of losing it altogether. Religious practice is, in fact, "the language" by which we express it and if it is missing we could end up in total loss.

If a person spends a certain time daily in meditating on the Gospel and in prayer, he is manifesting his faith. By this he admits that the light and strength he needs to live well comes not from his own thoughts but from Christ's life and doctrine. By Gospel study and meditation on the sacred text, he shows his inward attitude of faith in Christ and his readiness to let his own thoughts and whole life be challenged by Christ.

According to personal needs and, above all, as the love of Christ inspires, he will decide how much time he should give to these practices. His is the attitude of a disciple who knows very well that he cannot understand at once what Christ is talking about when he refers to his relationship with the Father, the necessity of carrying his cross, etc. But he is ready to listen and believe. Gradually his outlook on things, himself and God will become more and more like Christ's.

3. Time for intimacy

What matters is to acquire a Christian mentality, and this is not done in a day, precisely because, on many points, Christ's views differ from ours. Of first importance, consequently, is time given daily to Christ and to God all our lives through.

It will have special significance, whatever its form, for those in any particular way consecrated to God. They are in contact with him in other men all day long, of course, but in spite of the Lord's continual presence they still need to reserve time for this encounter, dialogue and closer union. Nothing can replace the need for close contact in the lives of persons consecrated to God.

Some think it useless to take time off to pray like this, claiming: "We have always to pray." This is certainly true, and for those who love God everything is prayer and a way to prayer. But those who pray continually and are in a perpetual state of mindfulness of God are precisely the ones who still take time to be alone with him. Why is this? Because at these moments intimate relationship with God takes on its full value. All that has been stirred up in the soul by meeting God in contact with men now becomes concentrated in the hours given to divine intimacy.

When a married couple has spent the whole day with friends, and their love has grown stronger in the cordial atmosphere, they are bound to long to be alone again. However much other people's company has developed their love, this cannot replace the need for intimacy for it to mature. The same holds for intimacy with God. For those dedicated to God and who love it is a necessity.

Such a mysterious sphere we can speak of only with great respect, for intimacy with God is each one's secret. God makes known his love and man tries to respond. If Christ had not invited us to receive this love we should have to be mad even to think of it.

The mere fact of recognizing and pondering on this love well deserves our devoting time to it in daily life; gift of time is gift of self. It would hardly make sense to declare that we loved someone and then not be willing to devote some of our time to him. During these moments we are uniquely present to him. In the same way at prayer we are present for God in the sense that we show our self-gift by total attention.

4. Human relationship and divine intimacy

Discovery of an intimate relationship with God unveils something unique that is not ordinarily found through human relationships. Some human contacts, assuredly, are so deep that they break into relationship with God and even sustain it, but there is always some part or quality of this relationship revealed to us only when we are alone with him in solitude.

The profoundest of human relationships foreshadows a still deeper one, and that deeper something we are led to through intimacy with God. But this is pure grace, for only God can make himself known; he is out of our reach. So much the more reason to be willing daily to dedicate time, however short, to attend to the divine mystery in the hope that God will grant us a glimpse and then an understanding of the singular character of his love.

People may sometimes be afraid that giving time to intimate prayer like this will lead them along some road apart from ordinary life. This, however, is an error; what is asked is not long hours of prayer but time of intense attention in faith to the mystery of divine love. And the outcome will be an intimate knowledge of God. Those brave enough to set out on this way will find immense inward peace and such liberty of spirit and heart that they will be just as human and awake to daily life as anyone else; above all they will be more themselves than traveling along any other road.

What matters in all this is the growth of an immense capacity for openness to God and to others. It should be no surprise if for a time the inward life draws us in on ourselves, though this should not be accepted as final. On the psychological level, mindfulness of the mysteries of God may effectively draw us away from contact with the world, but this is due only to the weakness of our human nature. The discovery of a budding love or preoccupation with personal problems may produce exactly the same effect.

As we shall see, the inner gaze is not turned to ourselves but toward a presence that is greater. As soon as we turn inward we should come into contact with the being who lives in us and is drawing us to himself in our very hearts. This discovery of the Other in us is already the dawn of contact with the rest of men and more particularly with those God has united to us by stronger affective links.

5. Self-seeking prayer and prayer as refuge

One of the strongest objections to personal prayer, as we have seen, is that it is selfish and makes us self-centered so that ultimately we are prevented from finding God. Solitary prayer, in this case, would be illusion.

We have already dealt with the need for particular attention to God's presence in us and our relationship with him. Here I want to examine our encounter with our fellowmen in our meeting with Christ. It would be clear that if a man finds Christ he cannot be far from his brothers.

Evidently, many who practice prayer are self-centered. They sincerely desire to relate to Christ, but in reality what they care for most is their own selves and their perfection. Thinking only of themselves, they want God to be equally occupied with them. But there is nothing spiritual in this kind of inner life which is simply a form of introspection.

In this context, solitary prayer becomes a way of living with oneself, taken up with personal concerns, not admitted as such but disguised under the pretext of perfection. This type of soul will say that he loves God and be convinced of it, though it will simply be a form of narcissism in which he thinks of God's gaze as mainly directed toward himself. He has become the navel of the universe.

There are others for whom the spiritual life is a refuge. Their soul bathes with relief in this peace in God. Desire for rest and quietude should not be too readily condemned. That a man should enjoy peace when he can is most natural. People look for it when they love each other. They want to be alone, and it is no flight from life's difficulties but a normal search for the peace, joy and love all men need.

Every Christian knows he can find peace and comfort in God. Christ invited his disciples to rest a while with him. On this point, fundamental Chinese philosophy is very clear. There is a time for rest and a time for action, a time for solitude and a time for life in society. This is the very rhythm of existence. Why should it not be expressed in the way we organize our spiritual life? There is a time for being with our fellowmen and a time for being alone with God.

6. Meeting others in solitude

What is most striking in all this is that, when in solitary prayer with God, we are also with our fellowmen. And what enables us to meet others in authentic depth is precisely being able to encounter God in silent prayer.

Sometimes contemplatives are accused of cutting themselves off completely from the world. They should mix more with people, so it is said, so as to know and help them better.

But there are many ways of helping the world, and those who withdraw to contemplate the divine mystery have a vital function to perform among men, for they are silent witnesses to the divine presence. They are those best able to remind men of the spiritual significance of the history of the world and their own. They may not perhaps directly proclaim the awareness of the divine they have acquired; others may be their intermediaries with the rest of men. But ultimately they are the real witnesses. Contemplatives secluded from the world are there to give tangible testimony to the invisible and to be a challenge to their brethren.

In all religions, contemplatives are considered to be those who truly know the world deeply. Their profound knowledge comes from the descending into their own hearts, which is to descend into the heart of humanity.

This idea is found among Taoist as well as other mystics. Lao Tze expresses this in the *Tao te king*, 47:

> Without going outside, you may know the whole
>   world.
> Without looking through the window, you may
>   see the ways of heaven.
>
> The further you go, the less you know.
> Thus the sage knows without traveling;
> He sees without looking;
> He works without doing.

The contemplative is not a separated man, but he relates at great depth to all things; he leaves behind the very things that separate and distinguish to penetrate the deeper levels of human psychology.

The position of a Christian on the way to God differs greatly from that of the monk of the Little Vehicle. No God comes to his help, and he has to set out on his own to seek the universal detachment leading to nirvana. As he leaves himself behind his road becomes ever more solitary. He plunges into the search for nirvana without even being able to desire it. For him, Buddha is only a wise man showing the way; he cannot be what Christ is for us. And there is no God for this monk whom he can love with an answering love. He is alone, alone and always alone, pressing forward toward knowledge but not toward love.

For Christians, love and knowledge go hand in hand. From the very outset of his spiritual life the contemplative knows both Christ and God through faith. From his first steps into contemplation he meets someone else besides himself, and this is Christ already living in him and in whom he lives. So he cannot simply close up on himself. Each of these steps is taken in and through Christ even if he is not explicitly aware of the fact. And Christ guides him to the Father and toward men.

This should make us understand why, from the start, the Christian contemplative is not alone in his solitude. Not for him is a narrow self-centered possessive egoism. Never purely intellectual, Christian contemplation is always a matter of love and therefore relationship. The object of knowledge in contemplation is God, who is an active subject: for he first loved us.

7. Reality of the partner
and truth of the dialogue in prayer

What has just been said will be rejected by those who hold that God can never be a partner in prayer, that is, in dialogue. They will call it dialoguing with self. In this supposed dialogue, they say, only one person questions and gives the answers, from which they conclude that it is pure imagination, and hence illusion.

Here we have to consider several essential points. First, God existed before I did, and I exist only by a relationship with him which was willed by him. I can no more deny this relationship than deny my own existence. Now the essential basis of "prayer" lies precisely in this relationship with God. In prayer I strive to become aware of it and develop it in thought, word and deed. Prayer, then, cannot be built up on an imaginary relationship.

Second, God is truly unknowable and I can express neither what he is nor what he thinks or wants. The great Taoist philosophers say of the Tao that it is *wu-ming*, "nameless." Yet they also allow that it possesses a name, *yu-ming*, because there exist manifestations of it by which "it" can be grasped. Of God I may also express what he has made expressible of his inexpressible being, and I could name it the whole of nature. More exactly, it is man, and therefore us, and, above all, Christ, the perfect expression of God. And I am myself God's image. Who can prevent the image from stammering out what it knows of its Creator?

Third, God has communicated of himself all that could be communicated and given by sending us his Word, the Son. After that he can say in truth that in his incarnate Word he has said everything he had to say and given all he had to give. Once more we are back at the objectivity of this expression of God. It is given, and it is for us to accept. We cannot cause Christ not to be: he is.

Fourth, it follows that Christ for me is someone who stands before me to express God and share his thoughts with me. Christ thus becomes essential to my prayer even if I am not especially thinking of him. As God's language he enables me to pray and saves me from losing myself in the mists of my own imagination. He is my prayer also, in the sense that he expresses my poor man's prayer to the Father.

Fifth, all this has no sense or value whatever except in and by faith. Without faith Christ's authentic personality would be simply a manifestation of purely human wisdom. God would not be visible in him, nor would he be seen to be God.

When, then, I see Christ I see the Father. As I listen to Christ it is the Father to whom I am listening. That is the basic principle. Even if I have plunged into a profound contemplation that appears to pass over the Son, I know, nevertheless, that in the essential reality of the relationship which unites me to the divinity, Christ is present. For he is ever the eternal Word, the only full and perfect expression of the Father, the divinity in its origin and source.

This will suffice to show that my relationship with God is not built up on illusions and that my conversation with him is not so many hollow words. For the very substance of my prayer is Christ. In this light my poor words and thoughts about God take on a depth of meaning; they become symbols and sacraments of a great mystery.

8. My meeting with all men in Christ

Christ, the presence of God among us, is also presence of all men in us, for us and with us. Physical presence, we know, is not the real presence. It may even produce aversion that is a barrier to true inward presence. Intense efforts are being made today to give men a deep communitarian feeling, which is a good thing that draws men together. But it has to be admitted that it does not do away with all temperamental and character incompatibilities.

Christ is the one in whom every man may be present to us over and above all incompatibilities. Just because he is for me the presence of the unknowable and inexpressible God, he is also the presence of all men, close friends or others. He is the universal brother in whom I contemplate the whole of mankind in all its breadth and history.

When Christ said that all one does for the least of his brethren is done for him, he clearly means to demonstrate that the position he occupies among men is that of the nexus and center of every human relationship. And among these there are widely differing degrees of depth and intensity. We are more or less bound to each other, depending on different situations, circumstances, social and family ties, friendship and love relationships. Hence, in practice, I have not the same degree of closeness with everybody. There are limits to be set and varying levels to be allowed for; otherwise life would become intolerable.

Moreover, if I take relationship with others at a deeper level, I can imagine myself related to a far greater number; I can forge links with others and so come to live a kind of universal relationship. When I think of myself as man I immediately relate to all men more or less closely according to my idea of what is in common between us.

Christ enables me to discover a still deeper meeting. He is not some abstract entity but a man who lived and spoke and does so still today. He wanted us to be all one in him as his Father and himself are one. When we truly meet Christ it is impossible not to meet all other men in him and by him. Christ, closer to us than we are to ourselves, who is "us," is also every human being.

If there is anything to discard when we meet Christ, it is self, and authentic meeting depends on this. Meeting Christ gives us to all mankind and all mankind to us. Ultimately, it is a brother-sister relationship, because in Christ we are all brothers.

9. Brotherhood in Christ

This encounter in Christ enables us to rise above all oppositions. The universal love we can reach has a very different quality or tone from that preached, for example, by Motzu. His universal love is something utopic that he claims can be lived in everyday life, whereas we know this to be impossible. Only a far deeper relationship can enable us to rise above inevitable conflicts.

But, then, of what use is it to meet others in Christ if we cannot live this out in daily life? Tend that way we must, but we must not dream of impossibilities. For example, there is a love between incompatible temperaments that can only be expressed through silence.

Anyone who seriously sets himself to lead an inner life should meet all men in his Christian heart; Christ is there in whom every human being is loved. We may be deluded and think and say we love, when it is a mere ghost of love, a kind of charity incapable of becoming active in deed.

An inner life and meeting with Christ should teach us to manifest the love belonging to the kind of relationship we have with others. We should keep turning to Christ to see how he loved and how much he asks us to love. The parable of the Good Samaritan is an example of this love: he suddenly loved the man he met by the wayside and in so doing he did all he could for him.

Then there is the love Christ manifested when he met the rich young man and called him to follow him. The Gospel tells us that Jesus loved him, with the deep love one can have for someone whose spiritual gifts suddenly emerge and give hope for the future. This is how we love in Christ—not only souls but persons, human beings with all their human gifts. Christ loved John the apostle, Martha, Mary and their brother Lazarus, and this affection was love. Through all these affections and friendships, Christ is our model and ideal of all human relationships.

Although never married, Christ set an ideal for married couples too. Paul understood this very well when he gave them as a model the love of Christ for his Church, since this relationship, lived and expressed in a specific way in marriage, aims at the same ideal as all love: to give one's life for the person loved. Again, there was Christ's love for Joseph and his mother Mary. He loved them deeply with all his human affective powers, but at a depth that still escapes us.

Thus our relation with Christ provides us with the stable basis for all our human relationships as well as affording a deepening and developing element. Authentic meeting with Christ enables us to actualize, each one where we are, the perfect relationship with others. In a real encounter with Christ lies the divine source of married life as well as every possible type of friendship. This universal love should unite all men, however much they may be divided in daily life and by different interests.

What matters is to grasp that anyone who goes into himself to find God may meet Christ who will open hearts and minds to understand and love all men in the greatest variety of relationships. In Christ and through him, I can most truly discover the love of the Father from whom all love, all affection and all friendship spring up as from their source.

V

Relationship with Men, Relationship with God

Modern theological and spiritual thought tends to insist much more on relationship with God in man than on meeting man in God. This trend explains the growth of communitarian prayer, seeking for God in sharing and witnessing to the love of God by human dedication.

All this is tied up with the discovery of man's value before God. Theology itself is moving in the same direction. It should, they say, start and not end from man. This is certainly a real revolution in Christian thought and a humanization of theology and spirituality.

Two words express this recentering on all that is human: personalism and secularization. Personalism here is understood as restoring his whole value to the human person.

If such are the trends, to build up a Christian spirituality for today will be impossible without taking this rediscovery of the human person into account. Now the aim of the spiritual life is mindfulness of, and meeting with, God. Have we then to go so far as to say it is impossible to find him outside human relationship and the discovery of the person?

To sum up one of the basic aspects of the problem, this is what a passage from a book on the new theology has to say: to center everything in man, as person, in no way diminishes God.

We should keep this conclusion in mind as we set out to elaborate a spirituality based on the rediscovery of man. Ultimately we shall be face to face with God, and the goal of the process, attention to his mystery, will be identical.

1. Rediscovery of man

I have defined the spiritual life as attention to the divine life, and I have shown how this is reached by mindfulness to our basic relationship with God. Furthermore, I have shown that this is perhaps more immediately achieved when Christ is seen no longer as the only mediator, the way, but as being one with us. Now it has to be shown that the spiritual life can be built up and developed by taking as an explicit starting point the person of other people, or the relationship between them and us.

One of the traits of our times is better recognition of the human person, a renewed consciousness that has deeply modified our outlook on the spiritual life. There are even those who go so far as to hold it impossible to attend to God directly. Only being mindful of our fellowmen could enable us to attend truly to God.

This is an aspect of renewed attention given to man advocated by Vatican II and developed in the *Constitution on the Church in the Modern World*. The Church wishes to show that it is more interested in persons than principles, in practice than ideas. As Cyprian Cooney asserts in *Understanding the New Theology*, "From liturgy to Bingo, from aid to foreign countries, to postage stamps, the Church and the world have to be centered on the person. People, not ideas, have to be at the back of our planning and ways of acting. People, not logic, have to be the basis of our problem-solving."

What should really interest the Church and Christians is man. But in this re-centering of everything on man and his problems, people no longer dare center their spiritual search on personal and direct union with God. Yet this attention to man is not meant to diminish God. The Church's intention is clear, but it is certain that this trend has given a blow to a spiritual life built up on more direct relationship with God and based on Christ.

2. Personalist view of existence

This tendency comes also from an existentialist view of existence. Less attention is paid to defining man from the ontological angle through the basic relationship that puts him into existence than by his actual position in this same existence.

Yet, as the Council states, the human person acquires his dignity from the fact of being the image of God, and each man is unique, absolutely singular in fact. He is a center of identity that can never be reproduced in series.

Every human being is one with himself, and this unity is at the same time his personal interiority. From this center of identity that he is, he is open toward a deeper center where he reaches still greater unity. Now this points to his origin which is God. On the other hand, the center opens outward and so is able to relate with other persons.

Each person tends gradually to become more "one" while weaving unceasingly closer relationships with others. Thus, each person becomes a center of convergence and radiation. He communicates himself and his mystery, and in so doing he receives the communication of the mystery of others.

Open on the one side toward God beyond the basic point of his own unity, and also toward other men, each person discovers that he is a way toward man and God. Such a depth discovery of the human person reveals a very simple and sure way to God. Simple, because it starts from what is human, and sure, because man is a concrete being with whom we can mesh contacts. And St. John stresses this when he says: "If he does not love his brother whom he has seen, it cannot be that he loves God whom he has not seen" (Jn 4:20).

3. Human relations and openness to God

This attitude sums up the answer to the movement of secularization of thought found in non-Christian philosophies. Christians stress an integral and truly existential humanism that puts man within the historical reality of his existence transformed by grace.

To take a Chinese comparison, Mencius, and after him the neo-Confucian philosophers, recognized that within man's very nature is expressed a relationship with heaven, but one that is not brought into the light of day. Hence, in spite of its openness toward heaven by the inner way, Chinese humanism remains very human. It even seems that for this very reason Chinese humanism found it difficult to take off for the heights we call spiritual.

For a certain Christian humanism, God appears plunged in the human to such an extent that the human itself has become a revelation of the divine and each single person is an incarnation of the Son of God, along the lines of "You did it to me" (Mt 25:40). In the world of Chinese Confucian thought, interpersonal relationship can with difficulty on its own rise to the revelation of God. Personalist Christianity will privilege interpersonal relationship as the unique locus of relating to God. We can well see what might happen to Christ with this attitude. There is no more reason for him to exist of himself, since he really exists only in his actual present and concrete incarnations. It follows, then, that it is an illusion to want to bind oneself to him directly, for this would be sheer imagination.

Parallel to men's relations to God in the Confucian tradition mentioned above is the highly developed thought of Buddhism of the Greater Vehicle. From this theory we gather that every man possesses in the depth of his heart what is called the nature of Buddha. This is present, not only in all men but in all living beings and every object. It is, in fact, the inner bond of unity between all that exists.

Won Buddhism, founded in Korea less than forty years ago, has built up on this principle a theory of relationship with Buddha himself which claims to be nothing less than relationship with all beings around us. Being good to others, uniting with them, we enter into relationship with Buddha. All that is human in itself becomes a revelation of universal Buddheity. This is the counterpart of the presence of Christ in each human person. In the Buddhism of Won, the nature of Buddha is not personal and hence it can be found in everything.

The notions of person and relationship differ very much between Christianity and Buddhism. But in either system, explanations respond to the same need to find a link between two such different and such infinitely distant things, the Absolute and the created being. This type of Buddhism has restored its value to the person and enriched it in a way that does not harmonize with the affirmations of Buddha on the non-existence of the person, the "non-self." But concretely this person does indeed exist, and if relationship is to be built up he must have a value. In the case of Won Buddhism, it seems clear that the Confucian influence prevailing in Korea in the last century is responsible for the reacquired value of person and relationship.

4. Interpersonal relationship and discovery of God

Ideas of community and relationship have made giant strides with the young generation so that everything is viewed from this angle. There are many reasons for this. The most positive are due to the growth of very strong bonds caused by the intensive structuration of society in modern times and the felt need to recreate human links in a world made more and more inhuman by socialization.

Traditional formality has disappeared or is on the way out. At the same time the person is left high and dry and has to create relationships that will allow development. Before, this growth came about haphazardly in a safe, closed situation; all that came was filtered through conventional relationships. But now people seek for direct personal commitment and the person henceforth risks being totally defenseless against the group.

For some temperaments this can be a terrifying thing, but it is good in that it obliges the person to commitment and relationships that are both self-revelatory and open to others. Through Christian personalism we have recovered a dimension that tended to be somewhat overlooked, and an authentic theology of relationship has developed, in the sense that relationship has come to speak of God.

I have already said above that the person is now seen as an incarnation of the Son of God. As it comes full flowering it is also a perceptible revelation of God. This is a far cry from atheistic humanism cut off from the divine. The mere fact that the person exists is God's revelation.

This is how we reach a revelation of God within interpersonal relationship. If the human person himself is an opening onto the divine, this relationship will become a normal way to discover God. Two persons having reached the height of reciprocal communication on the deepest personal level will find that their very relationship becomes a revelation of the One who makes it real. God himself—God as source, place, bond and nurture of their union.

5. Discovery of God in communion of spirits

In a chapter entitled "Friendship" in his book *Meeting God in Man*, Ladislas Boros gives us a very clear and beautiful picture of this discovery of God through interpersonal relationships. At the present time, a certain number of priests and religious women are preoccupied with this problem; it seems to them that their consecrated lives have cut them off from the treasures they might have had in interpersonal relationships. These seem the ideal way to come to a more authentic knowledge of God. Fear and narrow-mindedness have certainly blocked the road to a sharing of precious spiritual gifts. They have at the same time eliminated many illusions. If the path of interpersonal relationship is sweeter (which no one will deny) it is also productive of dangerous self-deceptions, especially when it is between man and woman.

Boros, in the above-mentioned book, begins by quoting the well-known description of what St. Augustine calls "the vision of Ostia." Augustine had lived for some years with his mother Monica in Milan, in northern Italy, and they were now in Ostia, the Roman port at the mouth of the Tiber, waiting for the boat to take them to Africa, their native land.

It was evening. Sitting at a window gazing into the sky, they were talking quite simply of divine things. Their intimacy had grown, especially since Augustine's conversion. Monica, unlike her son, was no intellectual, though her understanding of God's mysteries was very deep. In another passage of his writings, Augustine relates how his mother possessed a kind of natural grasp of the mysteries and the sacraments through her Christian faith, which her son took years to reach after his conversion.

There they were, Monica and her son, speaking of spiritual things and stimulating each other as they shared their intuitions. There was no trace of absorption in each other, only total openness of thought. Both were turned to God and each trod the footprints of the other to rise to more total knowledge of God.

Such a case represents the experience of a depth encounter, understanding and communion. The two elements, person and relationship, have reached their peak, and this gives the relationship its openness to the Absolute and its full human value. When we recognize the other as a person completely, we set up perfect interpersonal relationship. This can only open onto God, for the grasp of what is deepest in self and others brings out a basic feature of person and relationship, which is attention or mindfulness of a mystery half-glimpsed yet not fully grasped.

6. Charism of charity

One feature of modern Christian spirituality is the emphasis placed on the service of others. Service will become one of the most concrete forms of the love that the Lord asks us to cultivate after his example.

The Church has rediscovered in a new light, not the commandment, but the charism of love. We talk so much about Christ's commandment of charity: "Love one another as I have loved you" (Jn 13:34; 15:12). This order of charity, however, is not merely the observance of what we call a commandment; it has to be a charism. Paul saw this clearly when he said: "The love of Christ leaves us no choice" (2 Cor 5:14).

Inspired by a charity which was a special gift of God he could write the magnificent passage on charity in the First Letter to the Corinthians: "I may speak with the tongues of men or angels, but if I am without love, I am a sounding gong or a clanging cymbal. I may have the gift of prophecy and know every hidden truth; I may have faith strong enough to move mountains; but if I have no love, I am nothing. I may dole out all I possess, or even give my body to be burnt, but if I have no love, I am none the better" (1 Cor 13:1-3).

Charity here is something different from a gift of possessions, wealth or time. It is the love Paul will speak of further on that creates a true inward attitude toward the person we are helping and devoting ourselves to. An authentic relationship springs up between us and creates an essential inward attitude.

"Love is patient; love is kind and envies no one. Love is never boastful, nor conceited, nor rude; never selfish, not quick to take offense. Love keeps no score of wrongs, does not gloat over other men's sins, but delights in the truth. There is nothing love cannot face; there is no limit to its faith, its hope and its endurance" (1 Cor 13:4-7).

Charity here is service as well as interpersonal relationship. In fact, all Paul says expresses a person-to-person relationship where we are far from the level of mere service rendered or sheer utility.

What is interesting in this Pauline text is his description of the perfection of charity. This perfection should already appear in seed in its earliest manifestations that seem nothing more than gifts or service. Paul goes on to show very well how the perfection of charity is the actualization of total relationship with God, an intimate union in which God knows us and we know God.

7. Charity, manifestation of divine love

If the perfection of charity is intimate relationship with God it should also start with relationship with others; that, ultimately, is where divine charity is unveiled.

Paul continues: "Love will never come to an end. Are there prophets? Their work will be over. Are there tongues of ecstasy? They will cease. Is there knowledge? It will vanish away; for our knowledge and our prophecy alike are partial, and the partial vanishes when wholeness comes. When I was a child, my speech, my outlook and my thoughts were all childish. When I grew up, I had finished with childish things. Now we see only puzzling reflections in a mirror, but then we shall see face to face. My knowledge is now partial; then it will be whole, like God's knowledge of me" (1 Cor 13:8-12).

The last section of the text shows what goes to make up the greatness of Christian charity, an intimate relationship whose source is hidden, so that all selfless service or attention to others, expresses the deeper relationship uniting us to God. From this angle, service of others can never be a mere gift of object or time. We want to relate to the other person as friend or brother and in so doing our service reaches to the individual and unique reality of the person.

If this is the quality of our service it is quite certain that it is a path to meet God. In the very act of charity itself it is God we meet as we discover a depth we should never have reached alone. By actualization of the command to love "Love one another"—we come upon the other section of the phrase: "as I have loved you." Whatever we do for our fellowmen shows us, deep within our action, the active power of the love of Christ, and, in the one we are serving, Christ himself.

All the value and authenticity of a human act is there in our charitable deed, in no danger of illusion because we can see our brother. In him we relieve a physical or moral ill, or give a suffering man the support of our affection. Even were there no God or Christ, this act would already be of immense value; its human significance is what touches our contemporaries, and its intrinsic value is certain. To devote oneself for another human being, to show affection simply because he is a man, will also be marked with a divine value.

In normal circumstances, how can God better manifest his love than through what we do for our brothers? Our actions are winged with God's own love for us. We have to discover this significance; in so doing we find out what we are in the strict sense of the word, that is, God's presence and action in the world.

From this position, it is only a step to go on to conclude that God does not need our thoughts, prayers and sacrifices—and many have taken it. Those who think of this kind of secularized charity and service can work only for a humanity with completely walled-in horizons. For them, mankind achieves its destiny on earth and man will produce nothing more than a humanity unable to survive itself; but these are not the Christian perspectives Christ revealed.

In these, in fact, we see immediately that our relationship with God develops through human ones. For it seems clear that, without an experience of total, detached self-giving to others, it would be hard to actualize a fulfilling and robust relation with God. Relationship with God remains basic and essential; it is concretely realized in dedicated service.

A person might serve others with the simple intention of pleasing God. In this case, the contact through his action would be weaker than if he were convinced that the intensity of his human attention is the expression of God's attention to this particular man. He would then find God at much greater depth than in the first case. When we give ourselves in charity with a devotedness we know ourselves to be incapable of naturally, God shows that he is himself the inspirer and source of this love.

8. The charity of Christ

Charity that reaches the level of real charismatic power turns the intensity of divine love into mystical union. The charity poured forth in our hearts suddenly breaks out with extraordinary power. Christ himself appears to us seized by the immensity of the love union with the Father. It is one of the meanings of this inner witness the Father gives, for example, just before the resurrection of Lazarus.

Jesus let himself be asked, and then heard the prayer of the two sisters. Jesus' words to his Father take on a very strong meaning in this light. "I knew already that thou always hearest me. But I spoke for the sake of the people standing round" (Jn 11:42-43). He is doing it out of affection for Lazarus and the two sisters. Everything seems to be taking place on the human level, yet the love he is showing is the manifestation the Father has always shown him. Christ himself listened to Martha and Mary and let himself be moved by their prayers and tears. We can see quite well that the affection he showed to the two sisters and their brother is that of a human friend to friends. At the same time it is, on the human level, an expression of the unutterable love between Father and Son.

What Martha and Mary are asking is not a theoretical, distant demonstration of affection, like the promise of the resurrection on the last day. They wanted an active proof. This seems to be what modern Christianity is wanting too— not words but tangible proofs of love. John said to his faithful: "Love must not be a matter of words or talk; it must be genuine and show itself in action" (Jn 11:3-10). Most Christians of today are afraid of being accused of loving God with an illusory love and of loving others only because of this same illusory love of God.

But for many people an almost exclusive concentration on love shown in action is a way of escaping God's mystery in its nakedness which they find unbearable. It also supplies the security that faith no longer seems able to give.

9. The commandment of love

We should often come back to John's very strong words: "We for our part have crossed over from death to life; this we know, because we love our brothers. The man who does not love is still in the realm of death, for everyone who hates his brother is a murderer, and no murderer, as you know, has eternal life dwelling within him. It is by this that we know what love is: that Christ laid down his life for us. And we in our turn are bound to lay down our lives for our brethren. But if a man has enough to live on, and yet when he sees his brother in need shuts up his heart against him, how can it be said that the divine love dwells in him? My children, love must not be a matter of words or talk; it must be genuine and show itself in action" (1 Jn 3:14-18).

This passage "from death to life" is our conversion to Christ and our inner transformation by grace. According to the Johannine doctrine, Christ exists in his own life, but this cannot be separate from his existence in every human being. This is how far the incarnation goes. Both Christ himself and John ask us to look this great mystery in the face.

John follows up with texts on love: "If a man says, 'I love God,' while hating his brother, he is a liar. If he does not love the brother whom he has seen, it cannot be that he loves God whom he has not seen. And indeed this command comes to us from Christ himself: that he who loves God must also love his brother" (1 Jn 4:20-21).

What John wants to make us understand is the down to earth character of Christian perfection. This man who has revealed the secrets of God in Christ is the same one who puts concrete reality very plainly before Christians as a means of finding God. He is afraid that they may be satisfied with words and live in an illusory love made up of fine phrases and inflated sentiments.

John is echoing the words of Christ who repeated over and over again so clearly: "Anything you did for one of my brothers here, however humble, you did for me" (Mt 25:40). And recall this phrase which concludes description of the last judgment: "I was hungry and you gave me food; when thirsty, you gave me to drink; when I was a stranger you took me into your home, when naked you clothed me; when I was ill you came to my help, when in prison you visited me" (Mt 25:34-36).

10. Commitment and withdrawal in Buddhism

This notion of charity toward God does not withdraw us from our human tasks. It urges us rather to commitment. In Chinese Buddhist thought commitment to the world is expressed by the term *ju-shih,* and *ch'u-shih* signifies to retire from the world and not let it preoccupy you. Some people have the vocation of expressing *ju-shih* in an involved situation. Others express their life-style by *ch'u-shih*. The two tendencies should always go together, for it is Christ's teaching that if the two tendencies seem opposed, they do, in fact, meet. The man who withdraws from the world and its noise to live in the quietude of God should find solicitude for all men in his union with God. And the one who cannot remain alone before God in prayer may find God in every man he meets.

Before analyzing the relationship between the two commandments, by way of example, here are a few essential principles of Won Buddhism, a movement that started in Korea in 1916.

The manual of Won Buddhism states: "In Won Buddhism, faith is based on the following norm: 'Do everything to serve Buddha, because everything is the incarnation of the nature of Buddha.' This keeps all men faithful to Buddha all through daily life."

Then comes the commentary: The whole of creation is an incarnation of the nature of Buddha. Hence, even a blade of grass, a tree, a bird or animal is nothing else but Buddha. Each one has the Nature-of-Buddha. Clearly, these are the essential notions of Buddhism of the Great Vehicle (Mahayana).

Such a basic standpoint enables this up-dated Buddhism to claim to be the Buddhism of our days. It refuses to remain in the ancient tradition which corresponded more to *ch'u-shih* than *ju-shih*. The problem is no longer to retire into the mountains to find peace of heart and mind. With exercise, the Buddhist can discover in himself awareness of his basic identity with all things and every being in the Buddha-nature. When a man finds his "original mind" he will have no more difficulty in keeping perfect quietude or *ching* throughout all activity.

In order to reach this point he must practice assiduously the kind of Zen called *ch'anna* or *ch'an*. Won Buddhists repeat endlessly: "Everything is Zen, everywhere Zen. As in the teaching of Buddha, so Won Buddhism holds that the mind, in its intrinsic nature, is not disturbed by the environment, but by nature possesses transcendental wisdom."

We have wandered a little from our subject, but only to show the practical consequences of this deep identity with the nature of Buddha. It shows us the way Buddhists have solved a problem that obsesses the Christian world. This solution is a clue to their thought process and its divergence from the Christian mind.

11. The two commandments and relationship with God

Christianity is more caught up in concrete existence for two reasons: the incarnation, which gives fresh value to the human condition, and faith in the value of the person.

We may now return to the two commandments Christ left us: the first, to love God with our whole being, and the second, equal to this, to love others as ourselves.

In this chapter we have seen what might be called the way of the second commandment. Mindfulness of others, service, interpersonal relationship—all seem to point toward God, a way followed more willingly by our contemporaries than that leading directly to him. These ways should not be opposed as if they were two divergent paths. They are one, the two commandments being the expression of that same love rooted in the deepest recesses of the person and bearing fruit in relationship. Man's mystery opens onto the mystery of the Absolute and may become intimacy with God.

When deep personal love is totally unified and ardently participant in the life of the whole creation, it suddenly opens out to man and to God. But to reach this point is by no means easy.

Before any relationship with other men I was related to God. I was conceived in a relationship, and this conception is my essential relationship with my parents. With the life they could transmit, they passed on to me another and deeper life, a life too great and beyond their powers to give; they could only transmit it. They placed me in the vast life-current issuing from the Creator in which we are all immersed. Through the act which related me to them, they put me in contact with the source of all life, God himself. Hence, this relationship with God is deeper and prior to any relatedness to any human being, including my parents.

I can say that God is more my Father and Mother than my parents, which explains why the first commandment exists in a very real sense independently of the second. At the same time, by reflecting on what my parents are for me I learn to know God as my Father. Present, direct and immediate as is my relationship with God, I can only grasp it through a human one.

The total depth and breadth of relationship with others can come about solely through encounter with Christ present in every human being. If relationship with others can be for me the way to discover God, there will come a time when, it seems, man will teach me nothing more about him, but Christ will tell me a great deal more, both about God and man.

In short, God teaches me more of man than man teaches me about God. As I have said, a moment will come when man will cease to enlighten me on the mystery of God. The tide will turn and God's light in Christ will illuminate the mystery of man.

The day will come, I know well, when I shall have nothing to guide me on my way to God but God's own light. I shall be no more alone then than I am now on this earth. Relationships between us men will have reached the perfection of God's light; humanly speaking they will be more authentic than ever, but at the same time they will be more divine.

Then the divine light will illumine the human and so transform it that it will be the divinization John speaks of when he says we shall be like God for we shall see him as he is (1 Jn 3:2): realization of perfect relationship with God, complete and transforming knowledge, enabling us to be partners in love, as much like his Son as possible for beings which are not God. The Son himself is not simply God but truly man. And here, firmly rooted in his humanity, lies our way of access to the divinity and our own divinization.

Scrutinizing the origin of all things shows us the priority of relationship with God. At the other end of human existence it shows me that the day will come when every relationship will be caught up in the unique relationship with God. And when I look at the most beautiful of all relationships, I see it opening onto God himself.

Wherever I turn in my world, God is always there, closely bound up in its life and yet never enclosed in its boundaries. Human relationship expands into God but can never contain or limit him. God is everywhere, overflowing far beyond all our undertakings, all our powers or desires, in the vastness of his divinity. If the two commandments are similar, nonetheless, the first is always greatest.

12. To love the absolute love

However, in the practical, pedgogical order, the second is often the only one that fascinates man. True enough, Christ himself wants us to understand his "presence" in every human being and asks us to meet him there. The concrete existential character of the signs of love God asks us to give is very clear.

When John says, "My children, love must not be a matter of words or talk; it must be genuine, and show itself in action" (1 Jn 3:18), he is not merely offering a practical technique for manifesting our love of God, but expressing a theological dimension of Christian charity. These concrete disclosures of our love are not directed to God as to a secondary object, but they tend to "touch" God himself in the creatures to whom we show our love.

After speaking of the exclusive love of God in the Old Testament, Hans Urs von Balthasar once said: "Absolute love should be loved and exercised by the lover to the exclusion of all rival objects of relative love, which become idols as long as absolute fidelity is not maintained toward absolute love."

In other words, love of God for himself remains basic and should be the ultimate aim of our existence. This is the love that gives final meaning to every other kind of love. We have to tend to pure love, pure praise and pure service. Priority belongs to essential love. This is certainly the interpretation to be given to Jesus' reply to Martha when she worried about her sister Mary who was contenting herself with listening to the Master: "Martha, Martha, you are fretting and fussing about so many things; but one thing is necessary. The part Mary has chosen is the best; and it shall not be taken away from her" (Lk 10:41-42). In the same sense should be interpreted the last farewell meal offered to Jesus by his friends at Bethany. On this occasion Mary anointed the feet of Jesus with precious ointment and Jesus took up her defense against her critics; her act was a demonstration of exclusive love (Jn 12:1-8).

Authentic meeting of our fellowmen through an act of charity is a meeting with the absolute love of God. But, as von Balthasar says, we should see this in the light of God's love anterior to any act of our own. God loved us first., the initiative was his—"the love he showed us in sending his Son" (1 Jn 4:10).

To act as a Christian means to be caught up by grace into the divine activity and to love with God. Christian knowledge of God is only possible under these conditions, for "the unloving know nothing of God, for God is love (1 Jn 4:8). This text is sometimes interpreted as if the word "unloving" means simply the love of other men. So it becomes: whoever does not love his fellowmen cannot love God. But the comparison is between love and knowledge and not simply between two kinds of love. The love necessary to know God clearly includes love of neighbor and love of God.

If love of neighbor is proof and sign of our love for God, the love of God in its turn is the source and final end of all love. In short, everything should be placed in a total perspective of human existence. God's invitation to love was the starting point of everything; the discovery of this initial and basic love should be the ultimate goal of our existence.

And in the most trivial contacts of our lives we should be seeking and recognizing this same love.

As we end this chapter it is worth recalling once more that today's tendency is to insist on meeting God in others and manifesting love of God through our love of other men. We might glance at the attitude of Confucius who also insisted on manifestation of the virtue of *jen* that consists in showing oneself a "man-for-others." Though the Confucian school deliberately left to one side the question of relationship with God, it made the perfection of human relationship the ideal of the "way" (Tao). According to Confucius, the way is not far from man. If anyone follows the way and at the same time stays far from man, the way he follows cannot be considered the "way."

We have to be near men, and there we shall be able to reach the perfection of the way. We know well that in all we do we manifest God's "way" which is his dealing with men in love. If we are totally self-giving to others, we know, too, that we reach God, for the way of charity that comes from God goes to God.

Hence, the vital need never to lose sight of the source and ultimate aim of love: God himself in his very being. Truly God is hidden and inaccessible. But our inner life consists precisely in being mindful of the divine mystery in our daily living. This attention does not turn us aside from our concrete earthly involvement. On the contrary, it enables us to be still more attentive to the everyday task and the people we come across on the way. We are not distracted, but our attention has become deeper until it reaches the God from whom it comes. All this justifies total consecration to God for a more exclusive attention to the mystery of divine love, and of time given to silent adoration of God in prayer, a God so near and yet wrapped in impenetrable mystery.

VI

The Experience of God

The spiritual life is essentially attention to God throughout our life. The two preceding chapters have shown a double aspect of the encounter with God, one direct, the other by way of human charity.

Gradually it became clear that the spiritual life tends to set up an ever-increasing, deeper relationship between me and God. The value of my life depends on the reality of this relationship. But because no one has ever seen God, the contact will always remain mysterious. We are like people setting out in the dark. Each one asks his neighbors if they think this is the right road. Some who have already been this way can reassure us; others seem to possess an instinctive sense of direction. At times the group will stop to check up where they are; each will contribute his particular expertise. There are people who reason, others who share intuitions, and there are always those who have odd ideas or think they are very specially inspired. Pooling of ideas and experiences helps the group to assess approximately where it is and what to do next.

This is how it is in the search for God in the spiritual life. The whole Church is on the way and Christ with it. But however clear the Gospel words and example are, it is always a problem to know where exactly we are on our way to God. Christ has given us some objective standards by which to gauge if we are on the right road. Nonetheless, as soon as we try to weigh up our experience of God we run into difficulties.

Christ tells us that the proof of our love of God is the way we do his will. This is fairly easy. But if someone feels that in his prayer or daily life he has met God, grasped him in an unutterable way and tasted his presence, how is he to know if this is not an illusion or if, in fact, he has truly found God in a special way?

This is the problem we are going to deal with. It is a difficult one but is most important for the Christian life, and although it has many faces only those most basic to our spiritual way will be discussed.

1. Christian religious experience

Christian life is based not merely on mental adhesion. It implies actual experience, that is, an intellectual, affective, felt grasp of a reality ordinarily beyond the normal field of human experience.

Most often, conversion occurs after a more or less clear-cut religious experience. For some people, this will come like an almost tangible certitude. Others will receive a kind of sudden vision of the mystery, while it may come for some in the form of a specific emotion. It depends on the person. Andre Froissard, the former Communist, was suddenly converted when he perceived the reality of God through an intuition of what the spiritual life is. This is a typical example of religious experience. We had an intuition, that is, a grasp within normal human experience of a reality that does not belong to the ordinary field of perception.

In his book *Religious Experience*, William James describes such a sensation as "a particular feeling that seems to reveal to us the reality of the invisible." In other words, religious experience is specifically, the grasp of a reality outside the field of ordinary human experience.

As will be explained clearly in due course, this experience of God is possible precisely because it is not direct but is mediated through signs—signs that mediate a knowledge that outstrips them. God is reached through signs so that this experience seems to belong to the same order as any other human perception, and yet its object is not the subject of an experience like others.

William James' definition does not cover the whole of religious experience. It might even be misunderstood if it were seen as reducing the whole matter to a special feeling. In these things it is easy to be the toy of illusions. What can prove to me that such and such an experience is truly an apprehension of God? No absolute certitude of truth necessarily comes with this feeling. We are in an area where illusions abound.

We have, then, to take the problem as a whole and place religious experience on a wider basis. It does, in fact, involve the whole man, including his existence and activities; it is total experience, though it reaches its peak expression in a variety of ways according to the individual. For some, it will be a very particular feeling; others will have a vision; again it may be a touch or an intuition of total relationship with the Creator.

This religious experience is essentially personal because it means relating to God. In it, man enters into conscious relationship with the infinite Spirit who is God. But this, as we have said, should not be reduced to one single aspect since religion is an integral relationship of man with God.

Religious experience must be as wide as the field of religion itself. Man should undergo it with his whole existence and being. What is more, this necessarily personal experience is also necessarily communitarian, because we can only go to God and find him within our present condition. And even in our most personal activities we are bound up with others.

After recalling that religion—and, hence, religious experience—is both personal and communitarian, we have to see precisely what experience, and particularly religious experience, is in itself.

Experience is something we undergo or live. Hence, it is irreplaceable, and someone else's experience is no use for me.

There seems to be an infinite distance between abstract and experiential knowledge. What use is the description of something called love for someone who has never experienced it?

The current and over-empirical idea of experience makes it consist mainly of feeling. This is too restricted a view that emphasizes feeling to the detriment of other ways of perceiving that are basic to religious experience. To insist too much on feeling is to lay oneself open to being drawn into serious illusions.

We have to be thoroughly convinced that experience based on feeling and grasping may be mental intuition or perception, apprehension of a thought, strength of an act of will, impression made by a sentiment or understanding through an action. Religious experience may be still more fundamental and come about in the perception of God in that inaccessible point of our being which can be envisioned only in a flood of divine life and light.

It often happens that experience of God takes place precisely in a very deep zone of our being, beyond all feeling. This is such a specific experience that it cannot be put on the same level as ordinary ones. It bears the mark of its origin. But there is still need for correct discernment to recognize its religious character. This is a case of the most direct and pure experience of God possible, the type that is a feature of mystical states where the proofs are contained in the very experience itself.

What characterizes experience is here actualized: man fools the reality of God's presence or action. He experiences the reality of his Being. So something is felt—and it is the fact of immediate apprehension that is the sign of the experience.

2. Religious experience and faith commitment

When we say that experience consists of feeling directly, this should not be understood as pure passivity. If I am in a deeply peaceful state, I may say that I experience God passively. If I set out wholeheartedly in search of God, I have an active experience. In actual fact, as in every relationship, the two are continually intertwined.

So we can speak of both passive and active experience of God. Of course, God demands perfect docility and I can only lay hold of him by accepting his light and grace. Nevertheless, without a total commitment of will to realize this experience I cannot enjoy an authentic experience of God. To be real and effective, it must be both active and passive. Relationship with God is free and not imposed, and God wants me to go to him in an act of absolute commitment.

Religious experience, then, supposes a will-commitment in an act of faith. My belief in divine grace remains a free act, and I may set out actively along the lines of my faith to experience what I believe. At the start there is an act of pure faith and no experiential perception. As I go forward into a life that depends on my faith for its orientations and motivations, I accede to an experience that lies in the realm of faith, but which is already an authentic experience of the divine.

Anyone who commits his whole life to following Christ and living his Gospel already has a Christian experience. Psychologically, the feeling and experience elements may be slight, but such a life that embraces the whole man is already a religious experience. Actions and inward attitudes become true signs of attachment to Christ. Faith awakens fresh knowledge of him in the most down-to-earth daily living, and this becomes an experience of God when it enables us to grasp, in a still tenuous but very real way, Christ's active presence in the life of anyone who has given himself to God.

Here it is clear that total existence and not merely a fraction of it is basic to a religious experience, but this comes only through conformity with Christ in his Church and the community of men and supposes vital integration in Christ and absolute commitment. The life itself witnesses to the one who lives it.

3. Religious experience and man's freedom

Authentic religious experience is centered on under-standing and acceptance of the fundamental relationship between man and God. In this man discovers the source of his being—in other words, the basic unity of the human being. And far from alienating, this discovery unifies. It comes about through the integration of all the elements of the personality clustered round the understanding of the dynamic primary element of the person: dual apprehension that is relationship to God and unification and personalizing of man. There is an intellectual component here which in no way hinders the direct experience of the dynamism of the divine life animating my own existence.

Perception of my being-in-God leads me directly to my reality as person. In this sense, the experience of God is personalizing, for it is the integrating principle of all the elements of the personality. Such integration is expressed by the Taoist philosophers by the character *ning*, symbolizing the inner unification of the total psyche.

Although in certain states a man may be so struck as to undergo the divine action passively, religious experience usually needs a free act of will to contribute the voluntary element in man's relationship with God. Pure passivity might disintegrate the personality, and God has therefore provided for both a passive state with regard to God's action and at the same time the free act of man. It is similar to any other love-relationship—for without freedom love cannot be real love. Experience of God is, in its very act, an apprehension of human freedom.

This experience of God accompanying the basic act of my relationship with him cannot fail to react on me deeply. My very being is in contact with life itself, finding in it its fulfillment. Such a happening can give man an immense joy and exultation with a corresponding response in his whole being: when he meets God, man exults. St. Augustine and many other saints have described this inexpressible something which pervades the whole man, making every sense vibrate. God makes himself felt at a depth no man can reach, but from these depths rise up in mighty waves the joy of discovery and meeting. Thus does God reveal his divine love to us.

As we have already seen, the experience is both passive and active. It is also communitarian as much as individual.

Thus it is evident that experience of God is not an isolated fact in existence. It embraces all that is human in every concrete circumstance of this existence, which it then unifies and structures. First there is unification and integration, and then structuration. Total human existence and all the faculties are included in religious experience, and this happens in a concrete milieu—more precisely, within a Church whose faith and practice we accept. Within this life-milieu the experience will develop, sustained by the structure with its multiple elements that enable constant checking of personal intuition. Control will be exercised in the area of belief, practice and human relationship, and the authentication of my religious experience will be confirmed by the convergence of proofs, the most convincing of which will be agreement with the Church and my fellow believers.

The complexity of the problem is evident. A few essential points concerning experience of God properly so-called must now be re-examined.

4. Analysis of the experience of God

Religious experience is ultimately centered on the experience of God, the apprehension of the one who will always be the unknowable mystery.

This is the fundamental experience of religious life. In every religion man seeks to attain states that put him in contact with the divinity.

In some religious groups use is made of artificial means to produce states of trance or ecstasy that are supposed to bring about this result. There are sects which use intoxicating liquids. Today, drugs serve for ends not necessarily religious.

Extraordinary states of perception may thus be had, but they do not seem to lead to authentic spiritual experience or entry into communication with God. One may undergo extraordinary states, perhaps with hallucinations, intense feelings of fullness of personality or perception, but this is not an apprehension of God. Such a state of super-consciousness may indeed have nothing religious about it at all.

It is, moreover, always dangerous to give priority to these means which could lead to grave psychological disturbances. All such methods are based on the idea that human means and personal efforts suffice to procure extraordinary spiritual states.

Nevertheless, use of some natural methods may serve as preparation to communication with God. In this case, man does not imagine that he can with his own efforts experience contact with God. He simply tries to prepare himself and put himself into the best possible dispositions. This is something quite different from procuring extraordinary states by more or less artificial methods. Within the multiple experiences of God it is easy to discern certain more usual stages. These we shall describe in the simplest way possible.

5. Active experience of God in Christian life and meditation

Normally, we pray as we want, using our own words or feelings. We meditate on a subject by turning it over and comparing it with other similar subjects. Then we ponder these truths as we would any kind of problem, managing in this way to throw some light on Christian truths. This is the normal method of beginners.

In this case, we are aware that we are doing all the work, but at the same time we know by faith that God is enlightening us inwardly, believing as we do in what Christ says in his Gospel and in the teachings of the Church.

This is already a Christian experience because we are living according to Christ's teachings and in so doing we enjoy great peace and strength. All the problems of our human existence are solved in the light of faith, and we have thus an experience of faith within our existence since it is faith that conditions our life.

Yet God, the initiator of all these acts of prayer and Christian life, is neither perceived nor even glimpsed; he is there only like some invisible presence, believed in as here and active.

In the light of the Gospel and the teachings of the Church we try to understand God's ways. We interpret his plan and discover his love, projecting the light of faith on everything, but there is no direct manifestation of God in these events.

We could call this an experience of Christian life without direct experience of God. It is indirect in the sense that we believe in the real experience of those who saw God in Christ like the apostles, and in the truth of God's presence in his Church through Christ.

6. Passage to ordinary contemplation

Change of method, passage from meditation to contemplation, is a step toward more direct experience of God, for contemplation implies a changing inner attitude. In contemplation, man is more attentive to God's hidden action than to his own. In a very real sense the passage from meditation to contemplation is a preparation for more direct experience of God.

Notice that the word "contemplation" may have two meanings. There is a form of contemplation that is similar to meditation in the sense that it is a way of scrutinizing Christian truths, but instead of doing so by reasoning as in meditation, we try, for example, to imagine our Lord as in the Gospels; we read the text and try to be present at the scene, live with the apostles, imagine what they said or did. This kind of contemplation is as much a result of personal effort as meditation is and it does not suppose an experience of God. Faith still provides the elements of this contemplation. It could be called an entirely active, natural contemplation, like the meditation described above, but wholly immersed in faith.

Another sort of contemplation supposes a slight shift of attitude. It is the silent gaze or peaceful gaze. Each of these expressions implies a fresh orientation. Man reduces his own activity while waiting for God.

Reflections in meditation, perceptions in contemplation on the life of Christ, will diminish, and what is reached is often named the prayer of simplicity, dominated by simple thoughts and fewer but more synthetic intuitions.

The mind rests in these thoughts which by their very nature open onto the depths of the human personality. Maybe a person is unaware of being in communication with God or perceiving him, but he realizes that he is in contact with his deepest self. In this prayer, then, there is a kind of intuition of what lies beyond ordinary perceptions and thoughts, an awareness of the profound existence of a source from which his thinking is nourished.

Psychologists will claim that this source is the subconscious. Undoubtedly this is true, but it is not the ultimate explanation; beyond it unfolds the mystery.

What has been said of thoughts and intuitions may also be applied, other things being equal, to feelings and the basic attitude of the contemplative. He is no longer a prey to strong emotions but enters into very deep peace. This pacification of mind and heart is the fruit of simplification of feelings and emotions, a state of peace and rest highly sought after by all contemplatives and one of the characteristics of Chinese spirituality.

Closely related to this is the Buddhist desire for liberation. For Buddhists, the world is the cause of our spiritual impurities and the source of our troubles. So they first seek for a peace that is detachment from the cares of this world.

But this inner peace has a deep meaning, for it places us in a receptive state with regard to the mystery of the beyond. We rest in a very obscure perception of the existence of a reality far from the world we know. In this light, such peace prepares us for more direct experience of the divine. This detachment from the preoccupations that prevent our being attentive to the mystery is not yet apparently the result of God's nearness, but it prepares us for this approach. For the Buddhists, peace is not a disposition for encounter with God, but liberation from the cares of this world. Its religious sense orientates toward the final state of liberation or nirvana. In

Zen too, peace is connected with the experience of emptiness that prepares for illumination through the realization of one's most real, deepest self.

So far we are still in the area of ordinary relations with God, and there has been, up to now, no direct experience. From the peace we feel we are better able to ponder on the divine presence, but our inference still has to be based almost entirely on faith. At the same time there is already the beginning of a presentiment of the beyond which is a very tenuous perception, made up almost entirely of vivid faith.

The simplicity of thought and feeling and the deep peace of this prayer are the result of progressive simplification of activity in prayer. In the end it amounts to the final stage of a natural evolution of so-called active prayer.

7. Mystical contemplation

In the life of the contemplative there may come about a revolution. It can happen that as he prays silently, a man will perceive a mysterious presence which may sometimes seem localized, inside or outside, and sometimes not. What is essential to this new experience is the perception of something other than myself that appears to be the presence of God himself.

We perceive this presence just as we do any other, the only difference being that with a human presence we have no difficulty in recognizing what it is, because it is like our own. But here, since we have no direct knowledge of God, there is a difference. Nonetheless, we are aware that the presence perceived is a sign of God's own presence.

Ordinarily speaking, an act of reflection based on faith enables us to recognize this presence as a manifestation of God. How is it that the one experiencing concludes that God is showing himself? Logic is no help to this conclusion, but it is the interpretation of a perception that, acted on by faith, becomes ever clearer. Faith then gives meaning to an experience of human knowledge by letting us glimpse confusedly that this presence is a sign God gives his presence.

At the start, this perception of divine presence often co-exists with doubts as to how it can be possible. And yet in the depths of his heart a man is certain that God is there. Here we have a true experience of God. Normally it will grow clearer until God's presence becomes so evident that finally one day all doubts about its reality will vanish.

But where are the proofs? The experience, we could say, bears its own marks of authencity in itself—a criterion, however, difficult to apply. There are many who think they have revelations or visions when they are simply sick, so that their revelations and visions have nothing to do with a special action of God, but are only the products of an unbalanced subconscience.

If I were told that someone has had an impression of the divine presence, I would find it hard to judge its reality. I might say that it is quite possible but that he should not allow it to preoccupy him, for the essential is not the perceived presence but the One it manifests. By turning in faith to God himself, there no longer exists any real danger of illusion because a sign may always be used to help us to feelings of adoration and love of God.

Such an experience, manifested through sensible things, is apparently very human, and it often goes together with deep feeling and strong emotion. Again, this is nothing to worry about. If we remain unattached to these feelings they will be a help to greater consciousness of the divine presence.

Faith still gives them their meaning because the spiritual sense of these signs of the divine presence comes to us through faith. Signs are there for me to grow in awareness of God's presence in himself and in his action. Thus I give signs their meaning and I grasp God in faith through a human experience.

8. Discovery of God's presence

Although this perception of the presence of God is only a beginning, it is worth considering for a moment since it is the first step on the road to mystical knowledge. Man cannot imagine this divine presence but neither can he forego it; it can only be received. It is the first time in his spiritual evolution that he has experienced a divine action that puts him into a state of passivity. If now he no longer acts—or scarcely does so—it is not because he has simplified his prayer but because he has been silenced and drawn to passivity by the intense feeling of the divine presence. It may become so powerful as to absorb him completely. No more able, as in the past, to ponder on the mysteries, he is wholly taken up with a relationship to God that no longer needs outward proofs. Perception of the presence is its own witness to authenticity. He feels, sees, and knows that he is totally plunged into God whose divine presence invades him on all sides.

Such an experience of presence is a great deal stronger than any we could meet with in friendship, because it is both inside and outside at the same time—total communion in silence, reciprocal communication apparently motionless. A man finds himself wholly related to God in an existential attention.

Body, heart and mind are plunged in quietude. There is deepest peace in a contact that fills the whole being with an inexpressible sense of fullness never before known. There is no excitement, no violent fervor, only total conviction of being in harmony with God. It is quite different from devotion or fervor.

In our human existence there are many other profoundly peaceful and joyful experiences. What stands out here is that a person sees and knows experientially that this peace is from God. It is human, in that one sees, perceives and feels, but with the specific feature that its deepest meaning is spiritual. It is wholly evident that it is a concrete experience of intimate relationship with God.

9. Discernment of the divine action

Where, then, does final certitude come from? Some people, fearful of illusion, hesitate to enjoy this peace and have this experience. In this case they would do well to have a spiritual guide. One can gradually learn to judge one's own experience without fear of delusion by being always attentive to God beyond the signs of his presence, but, for this, time and patience and above all a balanced judgment are needed.

Taken alone, the feeling of peace may be deceptive; the ultimate criterion is life as a whole and its conformity with Christ, so that experience of God, which has its own intrinsic value, cannot be separated from the God-given witness of my life's total assimilation with his. Would-be mystical experiences outside the general life-framework could lead to terrible illusions. In this matter, more or less artificial means used to procure states of super- consciousness are misleading and the states produced have no connection with authentic relationship with God.

As with every step in the growth of an interpersonal relationship, so with experimental knowledge of God. A discovery made in an unexpected meeting has then to be integrated into the life-situation. Hence, in this kind of experience of God, we should be cautious and not jump to conclusions too readily. To be sure of the uprightness of our own judgment, we need to consult persons more advanced in spiritual experience.

We shall learn gradually to discern for ourselves how God enters in contact with us. But the signs of divine action will not be the same for everyone in the sense that they have a very personal value for each. They become ever more full of meaning as the intimacy grows.

The role of the spiritual master should therefore be very discreet so as not to distort the disciple's interpretation of the divine action. Attentive to the wholly personal character of the relationship, he should help his disciple to discern for himself what comes from God.

One of the outstanding signs of divine action is inward peace—no mere inner tranquillity, but a total existential manifestation of a profound harmony with God and all things, the flowering of a depth union whose effects rise up into the mind and feelings. As I have said, it is essentially the certitude of being in total accord with God.

Something quite different from a mere feeling of being liberated from the cares of life, it is, rather, a positive sign of God's action. This supposes that the events of our existence have the value of theological signs—they speak to us of God and are one of his innumerable languages.

God's presence is manifested in many other signs; in joy, for example—an inner joy that is not the same thing as peace. Inner joy adds an element of happiness and exultation that becomes more evident when God shows himself more explicitly than in the gift of his presence. One may, in fact, experience a great feeling of peace without necessarily experiencing a feeling of joy.

Although the final proof of the reality of this experience is life taken as a whole and its conformity to Christ, God does, however, often make himself felt lovingly to people who are far from being perfect Christians. This is one way God uses to touch deeply people who are tempted to turn away from him and who, maybe unconsciously, refuse to respond to his love. It is a grace he also gives to sinners. Hence, the gift of the divine presence is not necessarily bound up with a perfect Christian life. We have only to think of the great conversions, like Paul's, which came about precisely in the meeting of God with a sinner. Nor should we forget God's words to the prophet Hosea: "I will woo her. I will go with her into the wilderness and comfort her" (2:14). What greater seduction is there than the sudden discovery of the loving presence of God? So far we have described the appearance and development of this presence in the evolution of the spiritual life, but there are many other ways God can make himself known. We shall now go back to analyze the experience of the divine presence in the light of the evolution of the spiritual life.

10. Development of the perception of the divine presence

Awareness of the divine presence may take on many forms to which I have already alluded. At the start it is very slight, like a presence in the dark, but far more tenuous and stripped—the perception of an imperceptible loving attention that draws our attention.

When this presence appears, the soul has the feeling of something totally new and never before felt. Something is offered that is not conjured up by the imagination. It is the awakening to the perception of another universe as real as our own, and not far from ours, for it seems inside this presence, which is itself inside our consciousness, and our consciousness inside it. It is already a concrete experience of reciprocal intimacy. The person is aware that the presence of God within is an apprehension of himself in God.

At first, this presence may really seem impersonal, for the impression is as if the soul were face to face with a being so fugitive as not to be a person at all. A man will be overwhelmed by the mystery of this presence, immersed in it like a drop of water in the ocean or mist in the light of the rising sun.

He does not have to go in search of it for even without thinking of it he sees and perceives its presence. Should he be very busy it is still there, deeper than his surface activity. It is seen in the transparency of objects as if attached to their essence, which explains why thinking of it does not distract and perceiving it does not make a man less attentive to other matters. Like God in creation, it is a presence giving being and life.

11. When God's presence becomes direct action

Later on this presence may unveil itself as an active power. God seems then to operate on a man in a new way; he feels himself under the power of his action and hence put into a state of passivity. The divine action is evident, in such a way that absorption in God may sometimes deprive a man of all freedom of action.

In this case, the experience of God may be extraordinarily powerful. At times God may give a sudden intuition of mysteries. In a flash we perceive something barely half-glimpsed up to then. So strong a light leaves no doubt of its divine origin, for God alone can give such a perception of his mystery.

Again, God may manifest his love through feelings. The whole person is seized upon at an extraordinary depth and experiences an intimacy with God of which no one who has not tasted it can have any idea. Lost in God, he lives his love.

At times God may possess himself of a man's will to unite it to his own. Then he will give himself to God and be bound to him irrevocably. While God imposes himself on the soul, yet a man is aware of the freedom with which he accepts God. But this is impossible to describe.

No longer an obscure power bending over man, God is a personal force drawing him to accept a perfect interpersonal relationship. He has grown in an incomprehensible way and shares communion of life with God ever more intensely.

At this point, a man's whole life is one long experience of God, his every human action vibrating with the divine action. Such manifestations are as varied as human activity, and the lives of saints are full of them.

There exist, too, some strange experiences of God of which I do not need to speak here since they do not concern us. Enough that is essential has been said to illuminate the road of what is called knowledge of God in faith up to the first mystical experience. If someone understands how God acts when he begins to reveal himself, he is then able to interpret his experience of God when it becomes more intense.

12. Charismatic experience

We have already spoken of charismatic experience when dealing with the life of faith in Chapter II, but it might be useful to come back here to what is a widespread modern movement. It is part of a vast whole that should never be lost sight of, and like every other spiritual experience it needs discernment. Those who claim to be charismatics should not consider themselves exempt. Paul did, of course, write: "A man gifted with the Spirit can judge the worth of everything, but is not himself subject to judgment by his fellow men" (1 Cor 2:15). But this remark should not make anyone think himself superior to others. Paul is here addressing the still carnal Corinthians. There is always some danger or pretension in saying: "I possess such and such a charism." Gifts are not objects to be used at will; in other words, we have to go from the gift to the giver, whereas only too often the receivers of gifts become attached to them.

When Paul talks about the folly of the cross or the folly of the love of God, what he really means is a wisdom greater than that of Jews or Greeks. He is not speaking of some curious manifestations that one witnesses at times in prayer meetings. I may be deeply and very truly touched by the Spirit and let this profound grace awaken hidden powers in me that lead to unusual actions. This should be attributed, not to the Spirit, but to psychic unbalance. When people say: "Let the Spirit speak; free the Spirit," I may indeed be docile to his action, but I may at the same time be releasing the deep well of subconsciousness in the hidden recesses of my being. Then authentic experience of God might be carried off and submerged in a distorting emotion.

There is a fundamental rule of discernment applicable here as in all spiritual experience which says that emotion ordinarily hinders the depth of the intuition. Whereas some people associate emotion with depth, it is precisely what blocks the access to deeper spiritual experience. Charismatic experience ordinarily produces psychological and spiritual releases, which are difficult to separate. Thus, middling Christians have suddenly been changed by this inner outpouring of the Spirit, at the same time being opened up psychologically. Their problems and inner anguish have suddenly been swept aside and there is an inward liberation in depth.

Here different levels must be distinguished. I may assist at a charismatic meeting, be captivated by the atmosphere, touched by the charity, joy and peace I find there, and discover I am healed of my fears, and exclaim: "At last I have found love!" The mere repetition of a formula of praise may give psychological liberation and augment my faith in Christ. I may take this to be the Spirit's action, but this phrase is often abused, even to the point of taking all these methods to be direct charismatic action of the Spirit. In the full sense of the word "charismatic" it must be said that not all prayer is charismatic although the Spirit is alive at the heart of all the Church's approved or proposed methods. Taking into consideration the evolution of charismatic movements it is easy to see that they have elaborated their own methods, and like many others they also may become stereotyped. In this sense it can be said that such methods are a combination of the action of the Spirit and of man. Without making a sum total of these two forms of activity it is necessary to safeguard what could be called the autonomy of human action and man-made methods of responding to the impulse of the Spirit. To forget the principle of the divine action in man and man's action in God may lead to regrettable deviations. The Spirit's activity (and we should never forget this) is usually hidden in the very fibre of human activities, but to be always seeing or putting it to the forefront may easily be an illusion.

Conversely, I may receive a true charismatic grace that wells up from I don't know where in the depths of my being, a source quite beyond the deepest regions of my subconsciousness. Coming from afar, when it reaches the conscious level it is already charged with the clothing it received in the depths. This is why it needs to be discerned. To suppose that all that rises to the level of consciousness is a direct fruit of the Spirit is to expose oneself to great illusions, and we must be clear about this. The mere fact that one wants to allow the Spirit to act by letting go inner controls means that the current rising from our deepest-self is charged with everything it finds along the way.

So the great principle we mentioned in Chapter II remains valid. We have to detach ourselves from sensible and emotional signs so as to walk in faith toward the very source of the experience. Then it will be seen whether the source is superficial, deep, or at such depth that it silences us in adoration before the ineffable God. From the action of the Spirit, the power of God's action, we have to rise with and in Christ, to the Father, the source of all that is and the culminating point of the ultimate return.

VII

The Spiritual Life in Practice

In the preceding six chapters I have tried to describe the very essence of the spiritual life, namely, attention to the divine mystery of faith, which, if God wills to "speak" or manifest himself, may become an experience of the divine. This I believe to be the essence of the spiritual path.

Our human existence in every shape and form is involved in this spiritual experience. It is not just a section that would be added to the rest of our doings, but something that gives tone and meaning to our whole life. The question is: How do we get there? It is fairly easy to set aside time for prayer and divine worship in the same way as we keep space for music or sports. Some people look on the practice of religion this way, but the inner life I am talking about is something else.

It is not easy to speak of the practice of the spiritual life because its most vital and essential aspects lie beyond all methods. Yet, if we want the operating energy of the divine life in us, which is grace, to be effective, we must create certain dispositions.

The spiritual life defined as attention or mindfulness to the divine life will emerge if it takes on shape and is helped by methods. Those who practice Zen know this well enough. Simple methods to reach inner concentration do exist, but, that being said, it remains true that genuine attention to

God, a total existential tending, cannot be produced by methods, which are only helps. However, that is already a g eat deal.

In this chapter we shall try to give a few more practical directives which may help us to embark on the inner way. They are merely indicative and should be taken as such and not given more importance than they deserve. Otherwise they could impede the workings of the Spirit.

1. Conquest of a liberty for faith

The spiritual life, then, is attention to God and the relationship that binds us to him. In daily life I shall therefore try to attend to this relationship that is deeply rooted in my humanity.

Every religion teaches men how to free the spirit from outward, imaginative perceptions. When this liberation is total, the mind can apply itself to the pursuit of inner truth: man lives "in his heart," in the inner man. Such inwardness is common to all spiritualities in every religion and in some humanist philosophies, such as the Chinese.

In these last, spirituality signifies the culture of the values of the spirit, but without explicit reference to God. For the Christian, however, the spiritual life means very concretely a life lived in relationship with God.

The Christian viewpoint is human, but it sets up a relationship with God himself who is the absolute Spirit. Bound up with God in this way, Christian spiritual life may at times lose contact with the human, just as human spirituality may be reduced to an insignificant moral life, without depth or horizon.

True spirituality is both very human and very open to the divine. It goes beyond itself and refuses to be imprisoned in a heart that is not open to the universe.

Glimpses of our goal appear in Christ's teaching. He told us that we are children of God in a real, not a metaphorical sense. John very explicitly repeats this in his First Letter: "Here and now we are God's children; what we shall be has not yet been disclosed" (1 Jn 3:2). The mystery of our divine filiation is partly realized and partly to come, but it is ever growing and becoming more manifest. The locus of our spiritual activity lies here; this activity is based on an existing reality and tends to perfect it.

Faith alone can enable us to know this present reality and its perpetual becoming. For this reason we first of all have to make faith humanly possible for ourselves. This may seem an odd way of looking at things, but it is the only one. I believe in Jesus Christ and I believe in what he tells me, and I trust him without being able to explain to myself exactly why. What matters just now is that I take myself just as I am, with my faith such as it is. I believe, and I want to make this faith real, living and human.

And so I must first make my faith humanly possible. I know that my belief implies a choice, the reasons for which need not detain us here. For the moment I am on the practical level, trying to make my faith living, and in so doing it will become viable.

Faith is a fragile thing so long as it is not underpinned with our total humanness. Hence, I have to create such an atmosphere in myself that I shall be freed from incertitudes. Maybe there were reasons for them before, but now I have to go ahead with full conviction.

First, I must ponder the truths of faith over and over again until they become my daily food, flesh of my flesh and bone of my bones. This attitude follows on a now irrevocable choice, which justifies the undertaking of any believer setting about in search of the inner or spiritual way.

Such faith implies the kind of vision of a world permeated with Christ, the Word of God, who is its very heart. I have accepted this outlook as the only one that fits in with reality as I see it. Other aspects that might tempt me I will reject so as to plunge into the discovery of the way that seems the only one leading me to the heart of the divine mystery.

I shall free myself, then, in order to follow Christ this way. Some people would call this loss of liberty, but they are thinking of a purely theoretical liberty. However, in the concrete, "liberation" means choice and commitment. A man who would decide nothing on the plea that he might lose what he claims to be total liberty is, in fact, bound by a thousand ties that prevent action. He says he is free, but in reality he is bound hand and foot and non-liberated.

The choice of a life-orientation in the light of faith liberates us from a multitude of attractions that stand in the way of self-fulfillment. Christ said to the apostles: "The truth will set you free" (Jn 8:32). To him we have to turn unendingly, for he is that truth.

Natural spiritualities tell a man to turn inward to find his authentic human nature. His gaze must be liberated from the attraction of outward objects to center itself on the essential, his original nature. For him, the life of the spirit will be a continual return to what are called inner, spiritual values, since they are in the spirit and from the spirit.

In this light, the gaze will scrutinize the depths of man, and this inner contemplation will reveal man's relation to heaven or God. This return inward will produce essential liberation from secondary, outward objects. The true personality will then expand and man will live in the center of himself. Those who follow this road know how liberating it is. They know, too, that it is not to be acquired once and for all, because the outside world is always there to solicit and drag us down. Hence the need for continual exercise of the inner life of awareness, meditation and contemplation, all of which maintain and deepen this liberty.

In Christianity, anyone setting out in search of this inner life will enter into himself, but immediately he will find himself face to face with Christ, who is also a person. We know that ideals and ideas liberate us, but nothing is so liberating as a person.

The first step in the spiritual life, then, is to be present in affection to Christ, who faith tells us is the center of our life. This wholly spiritual and divine presence will have to be finally perceived and lived in the human mode of all our relationships.

2. Duty of reflection

To reach this point we have to come back again and again to what we know of the Lord, referring constantly to the Gospel and the experience of Christ made by those who knew and loved him more closely on earth.

In practice this means that anyone who wants to discover the spiritual life in Christ should simply take time off to read and study the texts that reveal him, above all in the Gospels. To decide to do this is not a fetter. It enables him to learn about the One who truly delivers him. The Christian does not withdraw into a corner to be alone but to meet the all-powerful Christ.

No doubt, our first steps will appear to be no more than a search for inner quietude, but that is only at first. The special feature of meeting Christ is that it coincides with self-discovery, for Christ is inside our human life. Though he may seem beyond everyday life, he is, nevertheless, immersed in it, plunged in it, but never to the point of being imprisoned or limited by it.

Practically speaking, there must be time for study, reading, reflection and prayer—not necessarily great lengths, but a certain amount daily, or weekly. To start off this might be Scripture study of texts and history, gradually attending to the meaning, what the text is trying to say, for it is the language of God. This should go on all our lives, and we can never say that we have had enough. Each period brings us fresh insights to strike us, and God wants these things to be made known in our times.

Then we should also go into the more doctrinal aspects of Christian revelation. Meditation then becomes a pondering on truths taught by the Church—its doctrine, the mystery of the Trinity, the incarnation, and so on. That could go on for years. It has this particular feature—that it takes into account not only the structure of human knowledge, but also knowledge by faith; for faith guides our thinking as we try to grasp the meaning of a God in three persons, or Christ as God and man. In merely human language this would be senseless. Human expressions of the mystery are excessively poor when compared with the reality they formulate, and we need to come back to them again and again in prayer to try to penetrate their deeper meaning.

Meditation aims at consolidating the texts so that the deeper perceptions of faith may have place. We have opted for faith and in its light we have to try to give consistency to formulas that have none for the unbeliever. If we neglect this reflection or meditation we may see the real faith content quickly fade away. Then, though our faith might appear intact, it could in reality be nothing but an empty shell.

Manuals of the spiritual life provide us with detailed methods and advice on meditation. They have their value, though they were given excessive importance in the past. Their weakness is that they could cause meditation to be considered a formal exercise. If I meditate well without distractions, I have therefore made a good meditation. Again, the temptation is often to take texts as subjects instead of truths, so that our gaze is not really fixed on the underlying divine reality.

When I meditate I ponder on thoughts that are the intellectual expression of a truth. In meditating on the relationship between the divine persons, I have to try to realize what this relationship in God can be concretely. I may possess a certain intellectual grasp of the text, but there is another step to a more efficacious mode of knowledge which is faith.

Reflection I make during meditation is still a superficial way of grasping reality in a more or less formal and disincarnate expression. After some practice I may still have remained on the surface of mysteries that I have never laid hold of in faith.

3. Contemplation

We have come now to what is called contemplation. The passage from one to the other is neither sudden nor radical. More often than not it starts by a simplification of meditation, with less reflection, less discursive reasoning and more intuition. At this point we can begin to talk of contemplation. Between meditation and contemplation there is as much difference as speaking of an object and looking it in the face.

Contemplation draws on faculties that are harder to define. It gives us a more vital knowledge of spiritual realities. These we try to see, touch and taste rather than make discourses about them. We draw on a particular mode of knowledge which implies the ability to apply our faculties to invisible realities that we can know only through faith.

What has been said of meditation is here to the point. Faith is an integral part of this knowledge. We gaze on Christ in his total being through faith, basing ourselves on what the Gospels tell us of him, and as we contemplate, we develop an intuitive knowledge that grows into an ever greater person-to-person relationship.

There is no need to insist, except to point out the importance of developing this more direct faculty of knowing. Though knowledge is, in itself, essentially a gift of God, since he alone can enable us to know and still more to make himself known, we should never forget that he has spoken to us in Christ. There is at hand a mine of knowledge in Scripture and more especially in the Gospels that should be exploited like any other source of human knowing.

The first section of this chapter was entitled "Conquest of a liberty for faith." It will now be more evident that this conquest of liberty is something other than detachment from the attraction of outward objects that normally fascinate our eyes and ears. What it really means is conquest of liberty by total commitment to the following of Christ, who is revealed to us in the Gospels, within my human milieu—not liberation by exclusion or separation but utter commitment to follow along the way shown me by faith.

4. Attention to God in daily life

It is difficult to persuade people that what is called the spiritual is not the intellectual, and that it can be lived in the most down-to-earth situation. God is present, not in some of our acts merely, but in all our acts. No single action of our existence is excluded from our spiritual life.

To concretize this truth, it is excellent to take the habit of never looking on our acts as human and nothing more, that is to say, without divine value. The human universe is so constructed that every action is performed in a divine milieu. It is not a question of expecting God to intervene at every moment, for that would mean placing him outside our existence. On the contrary, we should know that we are in God and he is in us. Our actions are our own, but on a deeper level they are of and in God. I am the one who determines them humanly but their resonance is divine.

To speak of a divine resonance means that these acts lie beyond the sphere of ordinary experience. It is as if they spread out in infinite vibrations beyond the limits of my experience. Conversely, I may, if I like, see the world I live in as closed, a kind of immense sphere, lying beyond in every direction, but still and always nothing but a prolongation of my own existence and the world I live in. In such a sphere, however far I go, I am always in a universe that gravitates around me, even if its immensity escapes me. This is the world of empiricism.

It is also possible to conceive of a world where, as I distance myself from the center, I feel a kind of liberation from its attraction, and the day comes when another center draws me. My race toward the infinite horizon of my world is going to become the endless race toward this other center. And that center is what I call "God."

5. Return to the heart and harmony

So here I am in my everyday life. With renewed attention I can turn to my heart and there discover my original personality. All spiritualities move naturally in this direction. The Chinese is marked by this tendency that reaches its full development in the philosophy of Wang Yang-Ming.

What many people look for in this return to the heart is no more than restful quietude. The fullness of peace they enjoy gives them fresh strength to plunge once more into action. There they will stay and make no attempt to get beyond this inward peace that gives back a meaning to their personality.

Others will take a further step. When they reach this palpable state of inner peace and relaxation they feel inwardly in harmony with all beings. Their interiority leads them to discover that of others. They realize that "person" means both self-possession and openness to others. In this discovery of the oneness of all beings in their deepest consciousness they are still on the level of human experience. Should this lead them beyond the boundaries of their personal universe to perceive another center of gravitation, it will still be of the same nature as their own. Practically speaking, we have to try to live the discovery of these person-to-person relationships by noticing others, trying to discern what they are within. But it is still the realm of self-culture without religious connotations. Just as in self-discovery, so when we perceive others, and in the relationships which follow, it becomes a closed-in network. Whoever lives this way, attentive to himself and other men and giving them his time, attention and help, will set up a web of more or less close relationships. This is the normal way of men in society.

There is another personal center for the man with faith, which is not an additional digit to all the human personalities. This center, outside our experiential world, we name God. It lies beyond the world of experience, but the road that leads there starts out from our human mode of knowing. The world we live in is, in fact, in God, and each one of the circumstances of our lives may be a springboard to a vision of faith to see this God. Our gaze, made possible by faith, is fixed on everything with the same intensity as any other man's but faith shows us a beyond. For everything has one, and if we let our eyes penetrate as deeply as possible, we shall come not on something but on someone, exactly in the same way as we meet a person in human contacts.

If we grasp this fact it will not be hard for us to understand what is known as the return to the heart, rest in the presence of God, contemplation of his mystery, docility to his light and finally, union with him in love. With these acts we can relate to him without ever turning our back on our human condition.

6. Human activity beneath God's gaze and in his strength

My concrete attitude toward what I have to do is also an opening toward God. When I have placed myself beneath his gaze, I have nothing more to do than try to solve my problem myself. I think it out, but before God, like a child who does his homework in front of his father. If I do this I know very well that I am the one making efforts to work things out, weighing each element of the problem. Faith leads me to believe that my life has an end wider and deeper than that shown by experience. The decision I take will include the fact that life does not end with death, that in Christ I have access to a life that is participation in God's own life, that the proof of the love of God comes through manifestation of love to other men. The list could go on indefinitely, for Christ has revealed an enormous number of facts about man's total existence.

By including in our search elements we hold by faith, we cannot deliberate outside this light of faith. We believe that this light is given when we place ourselves before God as son before his faither, disciple before master and friend with friend. In this way we try to apply in daily life those principles and precepts that we know only in part since they are from God. Even when we take all the great Gospel precepts, we realize that we know them only partially, for their ultimate motivation escapes us. In the final analysis, all this is an expression of God's will and love, and the divine will is personal. Here lies the basic difference between the divine will seen by a Christian and destiny imposed by heaven in other faiths. The ultimate explanation is love, and no amount of reasoning may imprison love.

When we come before God to try to take a practical decision, we are not seeking for a fixed and final destiny, but to relate to someone who loves us and wants to guide us to himself. This is the authentic mark of the concrete living of Christian spirituality. It reaches perfection when we are able to live our daily life in personal relationship with the Other we name God.

A relationship such as this will liberate man from the tensions of life and enable him to lean on God and rest in him—in silence, in the quiet of contemplation and equally well in the fever of action.

Many roads lead to this. There are people who one day have an intuition of suprasensible realities which are as concrete and tangible as the world around them. They are the happy ones. Others have to advance painfully along the way traced by Christ and all the great mystics. Day by day they have to ponder these truths, turning them over and over until they become as evident as the maxims of human wisdom.

The first will try to clothe their intuitions in flesh and blood while the second will seek to expose their human experiences to the light of the divine Spirit. Both will dedicate the major part of their attention to these mysteries.

7. Deep attention to the divine mystery

A few words about deep attention will be in order here. It is a very concrete aspect of the spiritual life. Meditation and contemplation methods need not be gone into since they are questions of practical methodology. But it may be very useful to talk of different levels of attention.

All of us have more or less the habit of living our lives on two levels. There is everyday life and our thoughts about it, for example, studies, professions, and the attention they demand. Then comes a whole world of inner thoughts that live with us and through which the deep life surfaces from time to time. Should this world not harmonize with our daily life there will soon be an imbalance. Where sufficient harmony prevails, we shall live peacefully and happily. On this level the thought of those we love is always with us.

We are aware that this thought is something more than mere thought standing alone; it is a deep, wholehearted, personal attention to others. However, its source, strength and very reality escapes us though we are immediately conscious of its presence.

This is the order in which relationship with God exists in an intensely lived spiritual life. Our very being is attentive to God grasped in the relationship uniting us to him. When the spiritual life has reached this point, it overflows onto our every daily action and finds an infinity of expressive outlets that a more formalistic piety will never know. The spiritual life is lived out day by day, actively aware of the love relation with God. The first intuition of God's presence following the act of faith has frayed its way in through the obscurities of life. Man has found the One who made him exist and causes him to live of his life. When he manages to live this life as consciously as his everyday life, he will have reached the perfection of the spiritual life.

The world of ultimate reality, normally hidden from man's eyes, has become the most real world. Not for this reason is our earth reduced to some insignificant illusion. On the contrary it has received its real dimension among all the things that have come to us from divine love. Living the spiritual life in this way, a man lives truly open-eyed to the totality of reality. It is the most existential conceivable view of human and divine reality.

In a variety of different religions, people live this spiritual life in their own way. Lived by a Christian it has its specific features, for meeting with the divine depends on no one's personal fantasy. Someone, a person, Christ, is at the origin of this tradition. His life was such that it set up the norms of a new religion.

8. Christ, our way and our life

Christ taught his disciples that in being attentive to him they were attentive to the one he called his Father. By adhering to Christ in faith his disciples could be one with God himself, and by living the life of the God-man, they would live the life of the God-God. The two, were, in fact, the same God. Christ showed how he himself in person was the complete solution to the problem of the spiritual life, that is, attention to God through relationship binding us to him and attention to our fellow men likewise.

Though attention to others may lead us to contemplate the divine mystery, Christ is par excellence the one in whom we gaze on the divinity, by whom we can enter into personal relationship with the Father. Christ is essential to our spiritual life, all the more so in that he is the only one who can put us into immediate, total, inward and reciprocal contact with the Father. It is he who brings about the inhabitation of God in us, and of us in God.

Now all this has a practical bearing on our spiritual life. Christ lived in history. He was the model and friend of a small group of people who are at the origin of a tradition on which we depend. At his death a Church grew up that gave body to his doctrine. Christ remains forever, living and active, and in each epoch he continues to make himself known in the here and now of history and concrete human existence. Both passing and eternal, this mystery belongs to us. Along the obscurity of our path our spiritual life should make us ever attentive to this mystery, and in so doing should prepare the vision to come.